ABOUT THE AUTHOR

Eileen Campbell is well known for her pioneering publishing and writing in the field of transformational change. She has written and presented for the BBC and is an experienced public speaker, giving talks around the world. She has written a number of books including *Guide to the New Age* (1990). Her series of inspirational anthologies, including *A Dancing Star*, sold collectively over 250,000 copies and are now available through her website *www.eileencampbellbooks.com*.

GW00371079

WAKE UP & HEAR THE THUNDER!

Finding Hope in a Hopeless World

EILEEN CAMPBELL

First published in 2012.

Copyright © Eileen Campbell 2012

The moral right of the author has been asserted

EC Books, Walnut House, Burgage Lane, Southwell, NG25 0ER

British Library Cataloguing in Publication Data. A catalogue record for this book is available from the British Library.

ISBN 978-0-9572386-0-2

Printed in Great Britain

Cover & book design by www.everythingevolves.co.uk
Cover photo by Colin Stump

CONTENTS

PREFACE

A monumental shift is taking place in the world in which
we live. Everywhere we can see the collapse of the
old order, whether in political, economic or religious
institutions, or in society and the environment, or in
science, philosophy and the arts. Our sense of certainty
and security is threatened as never before. We seem to
stand on the brink of economic meltdown, social unrest
and even possible extinction.

We're all too familiar with the bad news, but there is good
news too - a new and better era has already dawned,
though many have yet to fully recognize it. We are moving
from an Age of Uncertainty to an Age of Wisdom. No,
this is not some idealistic or utopian dream, but a reality.
All over the world a revolution is taking place, but this is
not just about the overthrowing of corrupt regimes which
we have witnessed in North Africa and the Middle East,
although this is part of it. Rather, this is a revolution in
consciousness which has at its heart a vision of humanity
and the cosmos that is holistic, instead of one that is
divided and separate. This revolution is about breaking
down the boundaries and about co-existence, it is open
for all to participate in, and it is made easier by the spread
and speed of the internet and social media. The signs

of change in this transition period are everywhere, as a groundswell of people of all nationalities, in cities and rural areas, from all walks of life, young and old are committing themselves to a different way of living and being which puts all forms of life as well as human beings at the centre of its approach.

The old era that was dominated by self-interest, greed and fear, born of a consciousness ruled by ego, is giving way slowly, and with the inevitable birth pangs, to a radically different way of life that is more altruistic, compassionate and sustainable. We are also witnessing the re-emergence of more feminine values in our culture, only previously in evidence when men and women first inhabited the planet and, with a very different consciousness from our own, lived in harmony with each other and with the natural world.

To us it may seem as if the world is increasingly chaotic and unstable as one crisis after another unfolds. In fact it has been that way for millennia, although there is growing view that the world is becoming less violent and more civilized. Harvard psychology professor, Steven Pinker, has shown how statistics reveal a dramatic reduction in death from wars, barbarism, murder and torture over the centuries. Others are also more optimistic about the progress of the human race, arguing that we are better off than in the past. Certainly in the Western world we are generally healthier, wealthier and have more choice and opportunity than at any time in history. But even in other parts of the world people are living longer, infant mortality is down, overall food supplies have risen, poverty is falling and technology is more widely available, with mobile phones becoming commonplace in some of the poorest areas.

Times of crisis are in any case also times of opportunity. What we need right now is a perspective of hopefulness, since without it, it's impossible to deal with adversity. And hope and optimism are out there, rebirth and transformation are possible – even against a background of disintegration. What is happening is much more about breaking through rather than breaking down, and it is part of the evolutionary process.

There are plenty of reasons for hope in this seemingly hopeless world, so drawing on ideas from a wide range of thinkers and disciplines, with examples of how things are being tackled differently, I suggest that the momentum will go on building into a new form of human existence. The crises we face are forcing us to wake up and participate in a future that is potentially more co-operative, more peaceful and more sustainable for everyone. We have far more power than we realize – to heal ourselves, our communities, our world. Our fate is in the hands of each one of us, and so is the future of life on earth.

ACKNOWLEDGMENTS

I would like to thank all the people whose work has been an inspiration to me, many of whom are cited in the bibliography. To others who have been my teachers over the years, helped me on the path and contributed to my overall understanding of what our purpose in life is, I owe an enormous debt of gratitude. I would also like to thank Sheila Crowley at Curtis Brown for her belief in this project, and Bill McCosh for his support and encouragement. Thanks too to Richard Beacham and Nick Brookfield of Evolve Creative Media, and to Colin Stump for supplying the cover photo.

There is nothing original in what I am putting forward in this book since I draw on the ideas of many people. We are all trying to understand these extraordinary times we are living through. I have endeavoured to draw together many different threads which give reasons for hope for a future that can most certainly be better and brighter than we might think at the moment.

'the peasant doesn't cross himself until he hears the thunder.'
Russian proverb

'All the crises of our age are manifestations of our challenge to consciously evolve.'
Tom Atlee

'We feel, many millions of us, within our cells a rising intuition, a yearning to be more, to create more, to participate more, to help more in the healing and evolving of a suffering world. And that spiritual impulse...is the impulse of Evolution, awakening in us – whatever our religion, whatever our faith, whatever our culture – transcending all of the past.'
Barbara Marx Hubbard

'...humanity has entered into a condition that is in some sense more globally united and interconnected, more sensitized to the experiences and suffering of others, in certain respects more spiritually awakened, more conscious of alternative future possibilities and ideals, more capable of collective healing and compassion, and, aided by technological advances in communication media, more able to think, feel, and respond together in a spiritually evolved manner to the world's swiftly changing realities than has ever before been possible.'
Richard Tarnas

'As bad as it can get, which is extremely bad, the course of human evolution may also be close to a phase shift that will see the fulfilment of our deepest and most potent dreams. Right here, now, on the brink of calamity, a real possibility exists that we will discover that evolution has been gestating in us all the creativity and wisdom needed to transform our most dysfunctional beliefs. Ahead may lie the alignment of inner life and outer action and the emergence of a picture of reality shared by both science and spirituality.'

James O'Dea

'Many of our deepest thinkers and many of those most familiar with the scale of the challenges we face have concluded that the transitions required can be achieved only in the context of what I call the rise of the new consciousness. For some, it is a spiritual awakening – a transformation of the human heart. For others it is a more intellectual process of coming to see the world anew and deeply embracing the emerging ethic of the environment and the old ethic of what it means to love thy neighbour as thyself. But for all it involves major cultural change and a reorientation of what society values and prizes most highly.'

James Speth

INTRODUCTION

The seemingly insurmountable crises facing the world today are all too familiar – whether it's the escalating debt crisis in the Eurozone threatening to overwhelm the global economy, or the disastrous effects of climate change and the disappearance of animal and plant species, or the soaring population growth putting pressure on the food supply. The growing gap between rich and poor, the exploitation of women and children, the abuse of human rights, terrorism and conflict – the crises seem endless, and none of us can claim to be unmoved by what we see unfolding on a daily basis in our media. Even in our privileged western society there are enough problems and issues in the world to keep us awake at night and make us wonder where it will all end. Events like the catastrophic earthquake and tsunami in Japan, the unprecedented (at least in recent history) events in the Middle East with the Arab Spring, or the extreme weather conditions causing both devastating floods and severe drought – all are profoundly unsettling. In the difficult economic times in which we're now living there is a sense of unfairness and injustice, a loathing for greedy bankers and over-paid CEOs, and a distrust of self-serving politicians. Around the world, from Oakland to Wall Street, from London to Bogota, we have had a growing mood of protest with the Occupy

Movement, which aims to initiate global change. No wonder the levels of depression and anxiety are increasing, and there is an overriding sense that all is not well in Western society, let alone the rest of the world.

All these crises however are symptoms of a world that may not be breaking down, but breaking through. Like the often-used comparison of the butterfly emerging from the chrysalis, we are waking up to the possibilities of a new life, a better human society. Overwhelming though the crises seem, good will come out of the chaos. Taking the long trajectory of history, and trying to understand what is happening at the deepest level, we can see that we are all being forced to change, whether we like it or not. It is part of our evolution, and we are in the midst of transition now.

In Part I, The Age of Uncertainty, I look at the stark choices confronting us. It's never possible to predict accurately what the future will be, and forecasters frequently get things wrong or fail to detect significant shifts. We can't simply extrapolate from the past given the extraordinary pace of change over the last 60 years, but the roots of the future are embedded in the present so we can map the possible social, economic, political and technological scenarios. From quite different perspectives – the worst-case scenario of breakdown and catastrophe, to the most optimistic and brightest of futures - we can have a sense of what might be possible and the changes we ourselves need to make. Preconceived views of the world can be challenged, old myths debunked, and new ideas embraced, providing we keep an open mind about the possibilities for change. We may then be better prepared for what may lie ahead and play our part in the unfolding of the future.

The catastrophe scenario is born out of fear. At times of overwhelming uncertainty people are inclined to believe the worst, and events can become self-fulfilling. In fact some turn to prophecy in their attempt to grasp at certainty. Rightly viewed, however, prophecy is a constant call for change, and there are many examples of this throughout history, as I explore in chapter 1.

In the opposite scenario – of a new dawn and a golden age – I examine in chapter 2 the nature of myth, and dreams of paradise, as an expression of longing for a perfect and harmonious world. Although this longing runs deep in us all, at the same time there is often a blind and naive faith that everything will turn out all right – we can just carry on as we always have done, things will move on and we can continue with our unsustainable pattern of production and consumption, have more, live longer and without any real effort or willingness to change ourselves. What myth does show us is the possibility of a different worldview, which is essential if our culture is to change.

The third scenario, which I deal with in chapter 3, is the most exciting and probable one, an evolutionary one – a shift in consciousness. If we look at the history of evolution, crises precede transformation, triggering quantum leaps in evolution. Evolution is not random, but ordered, intelligent and purposeful. Every time there has been a crisis in evolution, species seem either to have co-operated with each other or become extinct. New ideas in physics and biology indicate that we may be on the verge of making an amazing transformation in terms of the evolution of our species.

Evolutionary pressures seem to be at work to dissolve the illusion of separation which our culture promotes, resulting in human beings becoming more conscious of their thoughts and actions, and wanting to make changes to their behaviour because they understand that everything is connected in this great web of life. Empathy for our fellow human-beings is emerging as we realize that we are not isolated beings but part of a whole, and that co-operation, not competition, is the name of the game. The world appears to be developing her own cerebral cortex, a kind of global brain that connects everyone with everyone else, through the Internet and social media, and we are all now more easily able to communicate with each other and share ideas.

We've arrived at a pivotal point. The crises that confront us are in reality the prelude to the transformation of humanity to a higher state of consciousness. We can create a future that is radically different, yet more sustainable, fairer and capable of greater progress for everyone, both now and for future generations – if we so choose.

In Part II, The Age of Wisdom, I show how in our key areas of life – social, economic and political -   resistance to change is no longer a possibility. Shift is happening - new shoots and old roots are fusing together. New ideas and new technologies are helping to make us a truly global community, and the wisdom of indigenous and ancient cultures is once again being valued. There is a growing realization that we are all connected, and that what happens in one part of the world has impact elsewhere. No longer can we ignore the damage we've done to the earth or exploit those with whom we share this planet. It is early days yet, but there are many examples of people trying to lead their lives, run their businesses and organize themselves in less dysfunctional ways. There is reason for optimism because change is clearly possible and every one of us can play a part in that process. It is all of us who will solve our crises. The transition is already taking place and the signs are all around us if we care to look. The way forward is becoming clearer and we can take hope from all the initiatives that are beginning to transform our world.

However, without the most fundamental change of hearts and minds, new initiatives will flounder. A new society, a new economics and a new politics require that we all change ourselves, our attitudes and behaviour. To help in this process I offer in Part III my 'Wisdom Keys' for facing the future and healing the past. I call them keys because they open us up quite literally to a new way of being, one that is wisdom-based, rather than religion-based. They are what I have distilled from my study of the perennial philosophy found at the heart of all the great spiritual traditions as well as insights into the human condition offered by psychologists and philosophers. In a post-modern secular world, it is wisdom rather than religion that we can more easily relate to. The 10 Keys are the personal qualities, attitudes and behaviours that we need to develop in ourselves for this time of transition into the new era that beckons.

We live in challenging times and there may be even more

difficult times ahead, but it is not too late! We have a choice, and how we deal with the transition from one era to the next, and the kinds of decisions we make, determines how the future will unfold for us all.

PART I
The Age of Uncertainty – on the brink of change

CHAPTER I
Catastrophe - The end of time

Are we potentially facing the sixth largest mass extinction in earth's history, with thousands of plant and animal species being wiped out? Maybe a virulent pandemic, a nanotech disaster, or a runaway Black Hole? Could a bunch of terrorists get hold of a nuclear power station and blow up half the Western world? Perhaps a cyber super-weapon like Stuxnet could destroy our essential industrial facilities affecting everything from the supply of electricity to the water coming from our taps. Or could Los Angeles and Las Vegas disappear as Yellowstone National Park erupts and the rest of the world is devastated by fire and flood, as portrayed in Roland Emmerich's film, *2012?* Should we, if we're lucky enough to have the spare £32,000, sign up for one of Vivos's underground community shelters to get us through the first year of a post-apocalyptic world?

Our thoughtless destruction of the environment could well result in a scenario of catastrophe. Many argue that we are already seeing the signs in climate change with extreme weather conditions causing havoc. The global economic crisis is also causing, and will continue to cause, immense hardship and social unrest on an unprecedented scale. The rise of fundamentalism, the prevalence of greed and corruption in most parts of the world – all this can make us think that we are on the road to a complete collapse of civilization. Even in the arts a sense of doom prevails, from the sudden popularity of the nineteenth-century artist, John Martin, with his apocalyptic paintings, to films like *The Road*, based on the book of the same name by Cormac McCarthy, which tells of a father and son's journey across a landscape in which almost all life on earth has been destroyed.

Throughout history and across many different religions and cultures people have sought to know the future. There have always been prophecies about the end of one era and the dawning of a new one. In times of upheaval and adversity prophecy may be of some comfort, which is why people turn to it for it's a reminder of how fragile life is and reflects our longing for certainty.

Prophecies often seem to be linked with calendrical cycles, as well as with divination and reading oracles, visions and dreams and astrology. In many traditions, whether from North or South America, from the Middle East and Europe, or from the East, endless cycles of creation and destruction exist.

The Mayan prophecies are an example of this, and the ending of one great cycle of the Mayan Calendar on 21 December 2012 has been the subject of some debate. The Mayan civilization flourished for around 2000 years in the region of what is now southern Mexico, Belize and Guatemala.   Many aspects of the Mayan culture derive from an earlier civilization, the Olmecs, one of the oldest civilizations in pre-Columbian America and often referred to as the mother culture of Mesoamerica. The Olmecs seem to have had an exceptional ability for astronomical observation and making mathematical calculations and used a set of very sophisticated calendars (more precise than our own Gregorian corrected calendar) for planting and harvesting of crops. However, it was the Maya who adopted and enhanced the calendars. The Maya claimed that the founding date of their civilization was 11 August 3114 BC – the earliest date listed in their so-called Long Count Calendar, though this actually goes back to the time of the Olmecs. The calendrical system was in use between AD 250 and AD 909, during what scholars call the 'classic' period of the Mayan culture.

The calendar is both a cyclical and a linear calendar. The cyclical aspect was a sacred almanac of 260 days (divided into 13 months of 20 days each) which recorded the feasts and rituals associated with the seasons. The linear calendar was the solar year of 365 days (divided into 18 months of 365 days (divided into 18 months of 20 days each). Once every 52 years a remarkable coincidence occurs and the same day comes up simultaneously on both calendars. This cycle was known as the Calendar Round and formed the basis for the Mayan prophecies. Especially significant is the 400-year cycle the Mayans called 'baktuns', and the series of 13 consecutive baktuns called the Great Cycle – 5200 years. Our current Great Cycle is dated to end precisely on 21 December 2012, when Bolon Yokte, a god associated with both war and creation, is supposed to return. There are various speculative theories about other astronomical alignments taking place at the same time - the completion of an even bigger astronomical cycle of 26,000 years, known as the Precession of the Equinoxes. This is a phenomenon caused partly by the slant of the earth, and as it spins on its axis, because it's not a perfect sphere, it wobbles slightly. It's this wobble that causes it to move backwards each year – but only by one degree every 71 years, so it's hardly noticeable. On the 21 December 2012 the sun supposedly converges, as a result of the Precession of the Equinoxes, with the exact centre-line of the Milky Way (the Galactic Equator), and this is known as the Galactic Alignment.

I emphasize that this is all highly speculative, but according to the ancient Maya it is claimed, this ending of the Great Cycle will herald cataclysmic events. At the very least there will be a difficult and painful transition to the new era. At such times in the past, it appears there have been changes in global magnetic fields and climate which have caused sea-levels to rise, desertification and diminishing resources. The Popul Vuh (The Maya book of lore and customs) tells of three previous ages, each of which has ended in destruction. We are now at the end of the fourth era and will soon enter the fifth. According to the Guatemalan Maya Elders of the Eagle Clan, this fifth cycle will be one of wisdom, harmony and peace.

However not all modern Maya take the same view and many think the obsession with the date is misleading, and that it will merely mark the termination of one period of creation and the beginning of another. It's more likely to be a case of us projecting our fears of an apocalypse on to the Maya people. No doubt the date will come and go, as is the case with all prophecies, without a major cataclysm, the only real certainty being that December 22nd will follow December 21st!

The Aztecs and the Toltecs, who rose to prominence after the peak of the Maya culture, were very much influenced by them and have similar prophecies. Various Aztec myths describe four previous ages before today. Quetzalcoatl (meaning 'feathered serpent') is the great mythical figure, deity and priest-king (possibly even a real historical figure), who is supposed to return again someday, bringing a reign of peace and a new spiritual order after a period of chaos.

Native American wisdom also indicates a time of upheaval as a prelude to change. According to the Hopi, whose prophecies were handed down on sacred stone tablets accompanied by an oral tradition of interpretation passed on from elder to elder, we are in the closing stages of the fourth of seven ages. The three previous ages have been destroyed by fire, ice and flood. We are about to enter the fifth age, which the Hopi call the Age of Illumination. At the end of each previous age, human life was 'purified', and the Hopi have warned that once again we will see a 'great purification', or destruction. This is necessary because of greed, corruption and immoral behaviour of all kinds, which gives rise to violence, as Chief Dan Evehema, spiritual leader of the Hopi, proclaimed in a speech to the UN in 1992:

'Now we are at the end of our trail. Many people no longer recognize the path of the Great Spirit. They have, in fact, no respect for the Great Spirit or for our precious Mother Earth, who gives us all life. We were told that someone would try to go to the moon, that they would bring something back from the moon, and after that nature would show signs of losing its balance. Now we see that coming about. All over the world, there are many signs that nature is no longer in balance. Floods, drought, earthquakes, and great storms are occurring constantly and causing much suffering'.

The Hopi understand the world as a single interconnected system and advocate their way of life, with their concern for all living things, and emphasize the need to return to simpler ways of living and working in harmony with nature. This time of transition is known as an emergence and the Hopi have a ceremony in which they re-enact this emergence in an underground chamber, representing spiritual rebirth, recognizing that any change has to begin on the personal level.

The Seneca Indians also teach that there will be a 25-year period of purification leading up to 2012, after which there will be a new golden age. The Onandaga talk of a time when the water will not be fit to drink from the streams. This will be the beginning of the Great Purification, when there will be much suffering. Likewise the Kogi Indians of the higher regions of the Sierra Nevada de Santa Marta in Colombia believe this world (the 9th for them) will come to an end unless we desist from destroying Mother Earth.

As with other indigenous tribes, Kogi society has changed little in the past five centuries and they are very protective of their land and their culture, but now they are fearful of the land dying.

There have been other dire predictions ranging from asteroids hitting the earth to the earth's poles reversing. This is said to happen every 300,000 years. Apparently the earth's magnetic field has been getting weak and this is usually a signal of pole reversal, with all the dire implications that this might mean. Likewise the sun's magnetic field is also supposed to reverse in 2012. This happens every 11 years causing huge solar storms and more dangerous radiation levels than usual. NASA has warned that a new solar cycle is beginning (we have already experienced in 2012 huge solar flares erupting, triggering the strongest radiation storm in almost a decade), and this activity can have a disruptive effect on electrical power grids. Such storms are expected to increase in frequency, potentially causing a fair amount of chaos.

Eastern religions like Hinduism and Buddhism have their great cycles of creation and destruction. According to the Vedas (the oldest of the Hindu Scriptures) and their interpreters, we are now in the last years of the Kali Yuga. This age (so named after the apocalyse demon, Kali, not the goddess Kali) is the last of four stages that the world goes through as part of a great cycle of ages. Known as a dark age, Kali Yuga is characterized by greed, conflict and chaos, ending in destruction. The Vishnu Purana (one of the supplementary explanations of the Vedas) describes the last days as follows:

'Wealth and piety will increase day by day, until the world will be wholly depraved. Then property alone will confer rank; wealth will be the only source of devotion; passion will be the sole bond of union between the sexes; falsehood will be the only means of success in litigation; and women will be objects merely of sensual gratification. Earth will be venerated but for its mineral treasures...'(4.24)

Vishnu, the preserver god in Hinduism, has already saved humanity in previous ages, appearing as a saviour in many different forms. It is said that he will appear at the end of the Kali Yuga as Kalki, a white horse, the tenth and final incarnation, destined to destroy the present world and take humanity to a higher plane.

For Buddhists, and it's a prophecy found in the scriptures of all the Buddhist sects, a new and better era will be ushered in with the arrival of a new Buddha, Maitreya, following a period of degeneration, when jealousy, greed and strife would be prevalent. Maitreya Buddha is supposed to dwell in Tutshita, heaven, awaiting his final rebirth when he will renew the teachings of Buddhism. Exactly when and where is a matter of some controversy. According to one of the main pillars of Theosophy (an esoteric system of self-knowledge), Madame Blavatsky's *Secret Doctrine*, Maitreya is the last of the avatars (the form in which a deity descends to earth), and a great spiritual teacher. According to Alice Bailey, another influential theosophist, the Maitreya Buddha is supposed to return after 2025, whereas Benjamin Crème, another esotericist, maintains that the Maitreya is already with us.

Such prophecies also have their counterpart in the Abrahamic religions of Judaism, Christianity and Islam and are referred to as the End Times. All tell in their respective scriptures, whether the Old Testament prophets like Daniel, Amos, Jeremiah and Isaiah foretelling a time of tribulation and the coming of a Messiah; or the Synoptic Gospels of the New Testament telling of Jesus and his followers expecting the imminent arrival of God's kingdom on earth, preceded by a time of troubles, as in Matthew 24:4

'...see to it that no one misleads you. For many will come

in my name, saying, "I am the Christ," and will mislead many. And you will be hearing of wars and rumours of wars; see that you are not frightened, for those things must take place, but that is not yet the end.

For nation will rise against nation, and kingdom against kingdom, and in various places there will be famines and earthquakes. But all these things are merely the beginning of birth pangs.'

After Christ's death, the first-century prophecies in the final book of the New Testament, The Apocalypse of John, or Revelation, was written after John had been exiled to the island of Patmos. Full of symbolism and allegory, the apocalyptic vision of the end of the world and a day of judgment would be followed by the New Jerusalem - whereas unbelievers and evil-doers are confined to hell and damnation, the righteous are saved.

Likewise Islam has its prophecies of times of suffering and a day of judgment. Talking of the Terror descending, the Qu'ran says:

'... the earth shall be rocked and the mountains crumbled and become a dust scattered...the Terror shall come to pass, and heaven shall be split, for upon that day it shall be very frail.... On that day you shall be exposed, not one secret of yours concealed.... And those who have lived a blameless life will go to heaven; those who have not will roast in hell.' (Trans. By A J Arberry)

The Zoroastrian religion is one of the oldest monotheistic religions, founded by the prophet Zoroaster (or Zarathustra) in ancient Persia, probably around 1000-1200BCE, and this had a strong influence on the Abrahamic religions. It was Zoroastrianism that first taught the doctrines of individual judgment, heaven and hell, the future resurrection of the body, the last Judgment and eternal life. According to the Zoroastrian scriptures, the end of the world will come about when a comet strikes the earth. The Gathas (Hymns) tell of the Saviour, Shaoshyans, a descendant of Zoroaster, who will come at the end of history to fight on the side of Ahura Mazda, the god of light, against Ahriman, the embodiment of darkness. Defeating the forces of Ahriman for all time, he will renew the world, transforming it into a paradise of peace and truth.

So what are we to make of such prophecies and predictions? Are we on the verge of some catastrophic ending? In times of uncertainty, such as we're living through, it is perhaps not surprising that people look for something to cling on to. The doomsday scenario is however prompted by fear. The rise of religious fundamentalism is one manifestation of this, as is the prevalence of addiction, whether to drugs, alcohol, sex or any of the other addictions that abound in our culture. Much of the obsession with the superficial in Western society and the constant 'busy-ness' is an attempt to fill the gaping hole at the centre of lives that lack meaning.

The world is unlikely to come to an end - prophecies have continually failed to materialize in the manner foretold. In 2011 televangelist Harold Camping had prophesied that the world would be devastated, basing his calculations on numbers in the Bible), and many of his followers believed 21 May 2011 was their last day on earth. 'Apocalypse' is in any case a much- misunderstood word, for it does not necessarily mean some kind of cataclysmic disaster, but rather is about 'revelation', and the unveiling of great wisdom. Perhaps the only virtue of prophecy is that it forces us to look more closely and examine our behaviour.

Prophecies and calendrical cycles are perhaps best understood psychologically. We need to look at our troubled times in a much larger context. Our narrow view of time constrains us, but universal cycles of time can help us see things with clearer perspective. The great cycle of astrological ages, can for example, throw light on where we are in the process of evolving as humanity. We can learn a great deal from looking at the development of myth, symbols and religion in conjunction with what we know of history when we see it in the context of the astrological ages.

There seems to be a correlation between the astrological ages and man's development psychologically. The qualities of each astrological sign appear to permeate the religious values of an age. Respected astrologers and Jungian analysts like Liz Greene and Alice Howell have written on the astrological ages as applied to the history of man and have demonstrated the value of astrology and psychology in helping us to understand symbols and connection in life. Alice Howell writes:

'There appears to be an objectively observable coincidence of the nature of the astrological signs governing the astronomical Ages and the religious, mythic and psychological expression of humankind in history...' Each Age seems universally to be a stage in the evolution of human consciousness and the human psyche.

There are twelve astrological ages corresponding to the twelve signs of the zodiac in western astrology. Each astrological age covers a span of approximately 2150 years, and as one cycle of the twelve ages completes itself, the cycle begins again. Astrological ages occur because of a phenomenon known as the Precession of the Equinoxes. Due to the nature of the Precession of the Equinoxes the progression of the ages proceeds in reverse direction through the zodiacal signs. During the course of the astrological year beginning with the spring equinox around 21 March, the Sun moves through the Zodiacal signs beginning with Aries, then Taurus, Gemini, Cancer, Leo, Virgo, Libra, Scorpio, Sagittarius, Capricorn, Aquarius and finally Pisces, before resuming again with Aries. But the astrological ages proceed in the reverse direction, ie. Pisces, Aquarius, Capricorn etc.

Astrological ages make a very slow transition from one age to the next so there is generally a significant overlap when the characteristics of the new incoming age blend with that of the age that is waning. This is why it is so difficult to pinpoint exactly when one age starts and another ends, and makes for disagreement amongst astrologers. There is, however, general agreement about the core historical events which broadly occurred during the span of each age, or at least the more recent ages for which it is possible to find evidence via geology and archaeology (since the Holocene Epoch, the geological epoch which began approximately 10,000 years ago), and for the most recent ages via historical records. So, for example, The

Age of Leo (10,500 BCE-8000) saw global warming result in deglaciation and a rise in sea level. Since Leo is a fire sign, and ruled by the Sun in astrology, the synchronicity is fascinating, for it seems appropriate that it was during this age that the warmth of the sun caused the melting of the glaciers.

The astrological sign of Cancer is ruled by the Moon and is associated with the process of giving birth, nurturing and protecting. It was mainly a hunter-gatherer society at this time but it seems that some animals were raised and surplus grain was stored. The Biblical Flood may have occurred during this period, probably associated with the rising sea levels caused by the deglaciation of the previous age. There is evidence of the widespread use of boats, and as it happens maritime vessels of all types are ruled by Cancer.

Many archaeological artefacts – signs, symbols and images of divinities from tombs etc. - survive from the prehistoric period and throw light on this Age of Cancer (approximately 8000-6500 BCE). In Anatolia, the Near East and Europe, goddess figures have been found – round-bellied, representing the pregnant goddess of fertility, for example, the Palaeolithic Venus of Willendorf. Apart from cave paintings, these sculptures and figurines are the earliest works of art known to us. The figure of the Great Mother, as she is known – great because she gives life, nourishes and protects – is a nature goddess, originally worshipped in caves, and her priests were women. She was mistress of the mountains and lady of the beasts. Snakes and underwater creatures were sacred to her, but birds too symbolized her presence. There seems to have been almost universal worship of the Great Mother and the fact that large numbers of animal figures were found with the statues implies she was regarded as mother of all things. The society to which she belonged was earth-centred, egalitarian and non-violent. We know this from the striking absence of images of warfare and male domination. Instead the social order was one in which women were heads of clans or queen priestesses. Early man perceived the world mythically. For him there was no separation from nature, he was more part of a social group than he was an individual, and there appears to have been no differentiation between consciousness and ego. Early man was like a child, relating everything to himself and himself to everything.

The next age, the Age of Gemini, lasted approximately from 6500 to 4000 BCE, and a new kind of consciousness appeared, which allowed the potential for individual choice. The astrological symbol for Gemini is the Twins (two people holding hands, representing communication). During this age two important and significant things occurred to do with communication – first, the idea of writing emerged with cuneiform in Sumeria, hieroglyphs in Egypt and pictographic signs in India and China. Second, there is evidence of trade beginning to accelerate which helped with the communication and exchange of ideas. It would seem that during this age, the idea of duality and separation emerged as there began to be a split between the religious attitudes of those who began to settle and the nomadic tribes that continued to wander. We begin to see the first signs of organized religion in temples, art and artefacts.

During the Taurean Age (approximately 4300-2150BCE) nomadic tribes began to settle down and we get the development of agriculture and the breeding of cattle. As sufficient food began to be produced people began to live together in the first cities. As farmers planted and harvested crops they watched the cycle of growth each year and the first myths of resurrection began to appear. The astrological symbol for Taurus is the bull and during this age bull-worshipping cults began to appear in Assyria, Egypt and Crete. In this fertility cult the bull is the male instrument of fertility, but he is also its victim, being the chief protagonist in the hunts and festival games, but also the sacrifice for fertility. The Mother Goddess was still predominant and there were still mass burials in Europe and particularly in Crete, but things were definitely changing. The Pyramids were built during this era, bronze was used for the first time to make swords, and papyrus was invented – all of which have associations with Taurus.

As wave after wave of Indo-European tribes invaded from the fourth millennium BCE onwards wanting land for their cattle, the myths began to change, and the new gods were more human, heroes, some even bull-slayers. The Age of Aries (approximately 2150BCE-AD1), with its astrological symbol the ram, saw a very different Neolithic culture of small-scale agriculture and general animal husbandry, including the domestication of the horse. Aries being a masculine fiery sign, this is a much harsher world of conflict, the age of iron. Aries is associated with the metal iron and for the first time iron ore was smelted and worked into iron swords, replacing the bronze swords of the Taurean age. This is also the age of adventure and exploration and gave rise to the empires of China, Persia, Greece and Rome… The first attempts to replace polytheism with monotheism were made by the Egyptian Pharoah, Akhenaten, and there began the shift from the matriarchal worldview to a patriarchal one.

During this period people became increasingly aware of their own strength and their ability to use reason – a sense of individuality emerged, and so the separation from nature and mother Earth resulted in a projection on to a father god up with the sun in the sky. Man was now taking charge of his destiny, becoming self-conscious, and the hero in his own story. The ego had emerged.

The Age of Pisces, our current age, has lasted approximately from AD1. Pisces is a watery feminine sign and a dual sign, symbolized by the two fish swimming in opposite directions. An idealistic sign, it is split between the opposites of high ideals and spiritual aspiration towards love, selflessness and sacrifice, and the pull of daily life and secularization. Dominated by masculine values, it is the age of the individual, faith and superstition, and the great monotheistic religions - Christianity, Islam and Buddhism.

We're all familiar with the idea of the Age of Aquarius (popularised by the musical *Hair*) that we're now moving into. Most western astrologers date this astrological age from the 1960s that saw the rise of a broader spirituality with the interest in meditation and other religious traditions, as well as more alternative lifestyles, but it will not be full blown until sometime in the future. Meanwhile this transition period is one of instability and volatility as the new energies come in.

Aquarius is the Water-bearer, representing universal man, and appears to pour water from a jug, although this is symbolic and has more to do with mental energy, for Aquarius is an air sign. Aquarius is supposed to be visionary, and the age is linked with freedom, science and technology. It is also an age where we are concerned with self-understanding and the search for meaning. We are now seeing this in the form of the upheavals and tensions in our world, reflecting a deep inner change occurring in the collective psyche. We need to heal the split between mind and body, between the natural world and ourselves, and expand our consciousness. The emergence of a new tolerance, respect and understanding of all faiths will be a manifestation of this. No longer adolescents in terms of our consciousness, mature adults will evolve in this new age.

These great cycles are bound up with myth, religion and psychology. Over the last hundred years or so many respected scholars have written on this link (James Frazer, Joseph Campbell, Marija Gimbutas), looking at the evidence of archaeology (for example, burial practices etc.) and anthropology (social rituals etc.), and their work has been hugely instructive in helping to understand the development of the psyche in this larger context. It seems that at the dawn of history – in the hunter-gatherer period and during the time of the earliest simple agricultural societies – people lived in a relatively peaceful and harmonious way, with no status differences, no ownership of land or possessions, and with complete equality between the sexes. They seem to have had a strong attachment to the natural world and a respect for what they regarded as the all-pervading life force. And the mother goddess reigned supreme – the single source of life, taking her energy from the springs and wells, the sun and moon and the fertile earth.

Around 4000 BCE it seems this way of living was brought to an abrupt end by climate change triggering increasing desertification and putting pressure on the food supply. Competition for land resulted in invasion, violence and warfare. The Indo-Europeans, the Semites and the Hittites sought new lands. By around 2000 BCE the co-operative way of living had given way to a completely different mode of existence - war, patriarchy and social oppression, with the goddess now merely the wife or consort of a supreme male god, or turned into a martial deity.

This was not the case everywhere however, as Steve

Taylor has argued in *The Fall: The insanity of the ego in human history and the dawning of a new era*. Certain regions escaped this pressure and as a result continued to live in a more harmonious way. What is interesting is that this is exactly where we still have indigenous peoples with their different way of life, for example, the Aborigines, many of the native tribes of North and South America, the peoples of the Pacific Islands and some parts of Africa. Those indigenous people that still remain in existence today display the characteristics of this earlier time with their respect for nature, and lack of concern for status and wealth, an equal role for women, and a way of life that is simpler and less stressful psychologically than ours.

Another writer who has an interesting perspective on history and how humanity has evolved, in terms of consciousness, is Anodea Judith. A therapist by training, she has spent many years working with and acquiring a deep understanding of the chakras, the energy system well known to those who study yoga. She uses the chakra system as a metaphor for the evolution of consciousness and shows how from earliest times right up to the present day, each of the seven chakras represents a stage on the road the to full maturity of humanity. The Palaeolithic era was the age of the Great Mother. The Neolithic era saw a move from a culture dominated by nature to a culture in

which people dominated each other. With the Bronze and
Iron Ages ego came to the fore. In her view we are moving
from a culture based on the third chakra, associated with
power and the emergence of ego-based consciousness to
the fourth chakra, the heart chakra. The fifth, sixth and
seventh chakras are higher levels of realization, to do
with communication and vision, and although historically
we have moved through the eras associated with those
chakras, our development has not been consolidated
and we have remained stuck in ego consciousness. The
collective heart has as yet not been awakened. She sees
the heart chakra as 'the central integrator between the
upper and the lower chakras'. We have moved through
a vast sequence of cosmic cycles and are on the brink of
planetary consciousness.

We know that we're living in challenging times, and there
certainly seems to be a need for a dramatic change in the
way we live if we are to survive as a species. Certainly
the major threats to life on earth are caused by human
behaviour (asteroids and alien invaders apart). The global
crises reflect values, beliefs and attitudes that are no longer
viable. At their heart these crises are manifestations
of a deeper crisis – a crisis that is essentially a crisis of
consciousness, which has come about because of the
over-development of the ego, resulting in male domination,

competitiveness, greed and aggression.

The relevance of prophecies for us in our troubled times is surely best seen as metaphor, as a wake-up call to a deeper awareness of reality and the need to act on it. Adversity, pain and stress are often the result of old ways dying so that a new vision of life can be brought into being. Perhaps as the old structures that are no longer working disintegrate, we are at the cosmic tipping-point for change, where a significant minority of people who have been long calling for the need to change our ways become a critical mass. This significant minority might soon have so much impact on the current civilization that our current worldview of scientific materialism, with its individualistic ethic and its myth of separateness, shifts to a more holistic one in which heart and mind are connected, and a new era of sharing, caring and collaboration is born? Maybe we can let go of the old myth and create a new one, in which we come to see ourselves, not as separate from nature or from our fellow human being, but as part of one great whole.

We can choose to embrace change, working on ourselves to become fully mature human beings, for we are hardly that yet, as is evident from our collective behaviour which has so little regard for our fellow human-beings, the planet or other species. Instead we can leave behind aggression and competition, and constantly winning at all costs, and can work in co-operation with each other to deal with the crises. Let's not do what previous civilizations have done, ignoring the problems until it is too late, with the inevitable collapse of our way of life. Repeating the destructive patterns of the past doesn't really seem an option this time around. The Russians have a saying - 'the peasant doesn't cross himself until he hears thunder'. Maybe we've finally heard the thunder! We're waking up to the necessity for a radically different approach. We have an opportunity right now to respond differently, to change ourselves and the way we function in the world, and to make our world a better place for all peoples and all forms of life.

CHAPTER 2
Golden Age – the myth of paradise

While prophecy tends to look to the future, and usually to
a scenario of apocalyptic endings (even if prior to a new
era), myth tends to look backwards, often evoking a time in
the past of a more perfect world where paradise existed,
before the fall from innocence. Prophecy and myth are
two sides of the same coin, inextricably connected, for in a
sense both are an expression of our longing for a world of
harmony and a state of perfect happiness.

Myths are often seen as irrelevant and dismissed as legend
and fantasy, but the ancient myths of all cultures are of
value, even in our sophisticated, highly technological
twenty-first century world. Myths are in one sense
true stories, by which I do not mean they necessarily
happened as historical events, although it's possible that
they may echo in some way real events that happened
at an earlier time and were remembered (perhaps even
embroidered) and passed down from one generation to
the next as myths.   For example, the legendary island of
Atlantis described by Plato may once have existed before it
disappeared amidst the flood waters, some archaeologists
believing the Greek island of Santorini to be the origin

of the myth. Another example of an event that may have been mythologized is the destruction of Mount Mazama, a collapsed volcano in Crater Lake National Park in Oregon. The Klamath Native Americans of the area believed that the mountain was inhabited by Llao, their god of the underworld. A great battle was fought with his rival Skell, their sky god, in which the mountain was destroyed. In fact, geologists have proved that Mount Mazama was destroyed by a volcanic eruption and its caldera has become the second deepest lake in North America. Myths of many different cultures may well be partially explicable in such terms, but whether they are based loosely on actual events is still conjecture. More importantly, the myths are true in the sense that they convey a universal spiritual message that is beyond time, culture and belief.

For Joseph Campbell, the greatest exponent of the world's myths, they are 'the masks of God through which men everywhere have sought to relate themselves to the wonders of existence'. They are a kind of psychological road map, coming from the unconscious and expressing what we know deep inside ourselves to be true. They are existential in their truth. The themes of mythology are timeless, regardless of cultural differences. The same themes recur - creation, paradise, the fall from innocence, death and resurrection. They are stories we tell ourselves and seem to be about what we as human beings share in common - they are about the human condition and the stages of life that we go through. They also help us understand why things are the way they are and fathom out how to deal with the big issues in our own lives.

Myths help us to see and understand the fundamental unity at the heart of nature, which is why they continue to be relevant. For thousands of years human beings viewed themselves as part of the wider community of nature, interacting with plants, animals, mountains and rivers, as well as fellow human-beings. But today our lives are very different – air-conditioned homes and offices, cars, trains and planes, shopping malls, supermarkets and internet cafes – all prevent us from directly experiencing the natural world – we are separate and cut off from the sights and sounds of nature, whether it's the brilliance of stars in the night sky or the uplifting sound of bird-song.

Myths matter for they have to do with how we live our lives. They help us get in touch with our real selves, not the self that's influenced by our parents, teachers and culture. Mythic truths can help us today in our crisis-ridden world and in our own search for identity. When we question what it's all about and whether the life we're living is all there is, and when we ask ourselves who we really are, and wonder where we're going, we're asking questions that myths help us to comprehend.

Every generation needs to re-examine the ideas and values that have shaped our world, breathing new life into old myths and creating new myths. In our desire to explain the world to ourselves, we invent stories, myths and theories – they become our reality. The myths of long ago can help us give shape and meaning to our lives however because they arise unconsciously in all of humanity. Universal myths have survived and become the bedrock of all the great religions of the world. They proclaim a central reality and then build a structure of values around and in relation to it.

Myth enables us to appreciate the huge cycles of creation, maintenance and destruction, the eternal rhythm of the universe of which we are a part. In Hindu mythology the Great Trinity is a triad of gods, Brahma, the creator, Vishnu, the preserver and Shiva, the destroyer or transformer. In the cosmic dance of Shiva, he balances on one leg within a circle of flames, representing the continuous creation, maintenance and destruction of the universe, and indicating the perfect balance between life and death. Though his limbs move wildly, pervaded by cosmic energy, and his right foot is poised over a demon representing ignorance, it is the perfect stillness and serenity of the head speaking

of something beyond time and change that holds our
attention. It is only with the conquest of ignorance
that the attainment of true wisdom is possible. As the
archetypal dancer, Shiva represents the ever-changing
life-force with the myriads of worlds, galaxies and beings
taking shape and passing away. As the archetypal ascetic,
he represents the Absolute where all distinctions dissolve.
This endless round of existence means both beginnings
and endings – life renews itself continually. Things may fall
apart, but out of chaos something new is always being born.
Once we accept that there is unceasing change, there is
a deep sense of timelessness in each moment, the eternal
now.

Myths reflect psychological truths about the inner world,
often giving us the answers to the profound human
questions of who we are, why we're here and what the
purpose of life and death is. All of us will have experienced
something of a world beyond this mundane material world
in which we live out our lives. Dreams, music, poetry,
art and literature give us access to this other world, the
world of imagination. So too does nature. Even the atheist
cannot help but be moved to some degree by the beauty
and power of nature. Spiritual practice, for those who find
themselves spiritually inclined, whether prayer, meditation
or ritual, also gives access to this other dimension of our

existence that seems to complete us and make us feel whole.

We need to live in both these worlds – the outer, material world, our daily world, and the inner world of the imagination, the realm of the eternal, the world of mystery and soul. And it is in this world that mythic stories are of significance and speak their ancient truths. The point of mythic stories and symbols is not that we're supposed to believe them as literally true. If we try to make them the truth, they become dogma, with all the concomitant dangers that poses, whether it's arguing about how many angels there are on a pin-head or wandering into a crowded market with explosives strapped to the body believing you'll be reborn in paradise.

Myths can help us by showing a way to see the inner patterns in our lives. Much of the anxiety and stress we experience is because we have lost the sense of meaning and purpose, because we're no longer connected to the source of life. Myth springs from the collective unconscious, which has been aptly described as being like the common underground water table which feeds all our wells, influencing our values and behaviours. We are all unique with our own individual memories and life experiences, and each of us adds to the water table of wisdom. It is this which we need to be in touch with if we want to feel balanced instead of alienated. We need to feel fully part of the timeless universe, and connected to the natural world and to our fellow human-beings.

Increasing numbers of people are asking questions about our dysfunctional civilization as well as wondering about their own lives. Where have we gone so wrong? How come progress has ostensibly brought for so many of us in the Western world huge benefits, and yet we ourselves are troubled (only look at the huge increase in the number of people taking anti-depressants) and unable with all our resources to solve the problems of the rest of the world. Not only have we lost our connection to the world of soul, but we've also come to see nature as separate from ourselves and have reduced her to a mere commodity. Whereas the earliest inhabitants of the earth regarded every part of nature as part of the living whole and they understood that the creative life force ran through all things in nature and was sustaining, we no longer regard all life as sacred and have failed to understand that all species are interdependent and that our fellow human beings are our brothers and sisters. Perhaps the paradise myths are an echo of the more peaceful era when co-operation and equality existed.

Throughout history every culture has had its paradise myths, where human beings live in a state of innocence, happiness and peace. In Celtic mythology Tir na n'Oc was an earthly paradise populated by supernatural beings, a place of eternal youth and beauty, where happiness lasted forever. It has many similarities with Valhalla in Norse myth or the Elysian Fields in Ancient Greek myth. In Tibetan myth Shambhala is a mysterious hidden kingdom surrounded by a great ring of snowy mountains. It was the inspiration for James Hilton's novel, *Lost Horizon*, about Shangri-La, a hidden valley high in the Kunlun Mountains to the north of Tibet. This has so captured the imagination that 'Shangri-La' has become a common name for any kind of earthly paradise, sanctuary or home. The predecessors to Tibetan Buddhists were the people of the Bon religion, and they too had a myth of a hidden country – Olmolungring. There are other myths of hidden valleys in Nepal – Khembalung, and Sikkim – near the foot of Mt Kanchenjunga. The main theme of these myths is that someone stumbles on a hidden valley, but fails to appreciate his good fortune. Returning home to tell others about it, he never succeeds in finding it again.

This is echoed in the Chinese poem by Wang Wei (Tang Dynasty, 8th century AD) called 'A Song of Peach Blossom River'. Stumbling upon a hidden valley a fisherman finds a cave and beyond that, paradise. Eventually he wants to see his family and friends and returns home, but when he tries to find the valley again, he fails to rediscover it. Another Chinese myth tells of the hidden jewelled palace of the goddess Hsi Wang Mu. Situated on a jade mountain surrounded by a golden wall, somewhere north of India and Tibet, the palace is home to the Immortals.

The Hindu myth of Uttarakuru is depicted as an earthly paradise inhabited by sages and filled with magic fruit trees, some of which bestow immortality. It is one of the four regions which surround the mythical Mount Meru (sacred in Hindu, Buddhist and Jain cosmology and supposedly the centre of the physical, metaphysical and spiritual universes). In the Mahabharata, one of the great epics of Hindu mythology, Arjuna travels through the Himalayas to Lake Manasarovar at the foot of Mount Kailas, crossing the Tibetan plateau to reach Uttarakuru.

The Scythians, a nomadic people of the first millennium BCE also believed in a paradise which was located towards the North Pole yet had a warm climate, where happy and contented people lived. It may have been like the northern paradise of the Hyperboreans which the Greeks and Romans believed in - a land of perpetual spring whose inhabitants lived in bliss and harmony.

In the Jewish and Christian tradition the Garden of Eden, according to the Genesis account in the Old Testament, was a place of fruit trees, flowing waters, gold and precious stones. The Qu'ran's paradise is an oasis-like garden with trees laden with dates and pomegranates, watered by a central fountain and pure rivers. It is possible that the story derives from an early Mesopotamian myth, as there are close parallels to the description of a fabulous land in Sumerian texts. In Persian mythology (the word paradise comes from the Old Iranian word *Pairi-daeza*, meaning a walled or enclosed garden), the great King Yima, whose age was a time of perfection, had a paradise garden on top of a mountain where magical trees grew, including a Tree of Life, and where the water of life had its source.

The Ancient Egyptians also had a belief in a heavenly paradise, known as Aaru, where Osiris (god of the underworld), ruled. Rather like the earthly Nile reed beds, this was ideal hunting and fishing grounds where the dead lived after they have been positively judged and their hearts have been found to weigh the same as the ostrich feather of Maat (the goddess and personification of truth and justice). Similar myths occur in the very different traditions of Australia, Native Americans and African tribes: for example, the Aborigines consider that their mythical ancestors lived in an earthly paradise in which game abounded and the idea of good and evil was unknown; there is a Cheyenne myth which tells of a time of paradise when human beings were naked and innocent amid fields of plenty; and the tribes of central and southern Africa believed that people lived in the sky with God, there was no separation and they were happy.

Whether these myths of paradise are an echo of an earlier time in the history of mankind, or whether they merely reflect man's longing for something beyond this world of strife, where peace and happiness can be experienced, it's hard to say. It is possible that they hark back to an earlier time when men and women lived in harmony both with themselves and with nature before things changed so dramatically. Riane Eisler, in *The Chalice and the Blade*, describes the way men and women lived together in a primarily horticultural society with no rigid hierarchical structures or male domination, and the archaeological evidence seems to confirm this, whether the Neolithic excavational evidence at Catal Huyuk (one of the world's first towns built in Anatolia, the rich central plateau of what is now modern-day Turkey) or the Bronze Age ruins of Minoan Crete.

It's also possible that the paradise myths record an even earlier era when wild animals and plants were more plentiful. Palaeontological evidence certainly seems to indicate that there was once a time of greater abundance, perhaps prior to some great catastrophe such as a flood.

And perhaps the paradise myths are allegories – stories used by early peoples to convey important psychological truths. Maybe the stories of paradise are allegorical descriptions of the early stages in the evolution of the collective unconscious and reflect a time when consciousness was perfectly attuned to the world around. All was peace and harmony, but because of some fundamental mistake on the part of man - forgetting one's true identity (Hindu and Buddhist ideas), disobedience of God's will (the Bible) or fighting, according to many mythologies - perhaps this 'Fall', this loss of innocence, is due to the emergence of the ego, as many have argued. As the ego became more pronounced, a new sense of separation and alienation grew. Survival in this more violent world resulted in the development of a problem-solving intelligence which resulted in amazing achievements, but the sense of connection with nature was lost. In spite of the problems caused by the development of the ego however, there is no denying that it has been a necessary stage in man's evolution.

In today's secular and materialistic world gleaming with

remarkable achievements, there has been a tendency to think that paradise is about having wealth and all it brings. Progress and economic growth, along with technology, have been thought capable of solving the world's problems. But as the West has become more mired in debt, and the economic, social and environmental costs are beginning to be understood, and as the developing countries like China and India try to attain the same standard of living that we have enjoyed until now, it is clear that we are mistaken.

The myths of paradise gardens, hidden kingdoms and golden ages remind us that there's more to this world than we realize. The Qu'ran says: 'Paradise is nearer to you than the thongs of your sandals.' Swami Muktananda, a wise Kashmir Shaivite teacher, told a wonderful story about an argument between the gods over where to hide the secret of the universe …the long and the short of it is they settle on hiding it in the human heart since man will never think of looking there…. Similarly an old Tibetan story tells of a young man setting off to try and find the mythical kingdom of Shambhala. After traversing plains and mountains he finally arrives at the cave of an old hermit. When the hermit questions him about where he's going, the young seeker tells him that he is trying to find Shambhala. The hermit then tells him that there is no need to travel very far because the kingdom of Shambhala is in his own heart.

Just as Christ tells us in the New Testament – 'the kingdom of God is within you.' The essence of what we are looking for in all our searching for happiness and meaning, is the same essence that is at the heart of the universe.

Ultimately it's this connection with the eternal that we long for in all our dreams of paradise. Only that connection with the source of all life can fulfil us and bring us the kind of peace and happiness we desire. The paradise myths perhaps show us that if only we open our eyes, paradise exists in the here and now – when everything is seen for what it is, part of the whole, then life on earth is paradise, and we can hope, as William Blake suggests, 'to see a world in a grain of sand.'

There is also another group of myths, linked with the paradise myths, which it is worth exploring in trying to make sense of our growth and development as human beings – that of the hero's journey. Here again archaeologists, anthropologists and psychologists have been fascinated by the dramatic change that seems to have taken place in myth during the third millennium BCE. Whereas once fertility goddesses, nature spirits etc. prevailed, by 2000 BCE most of the prominent deities in Europe and the Near East were male. From now on mythology was about heroes overcoming obstacles, facing danger and vanquishing opponents. This probably reflected the more patriarchal and hierarchical society that developed with invasions and wars as a result of migratory pressures, as we have just seen.

The myth of the hero's journey is best epitomized by Homer's tale of Odysseus, the hero of the Trojan Wars and the King of Ithaca, and his return journey to his homeland through many a challenge and danger. *The Odyssey*, with its monsters, temptations, trials and deprivations is very much our story, a metaphorical story of self-discovery. All great stories have the power within them to help us change our lives. *The Odyssey* represents the life cycle – the young hero leaves home, encounters all kinds of challenges and finally returns as a mature, wise man. The youth often feels he is invulnerable, and powerful as the gods themselves, but is invariably punished by some kind of fall, as a result of which he has to learn the lesson of false pride. The heroic cycle shares characteristics with many other wonderful myths and stories from other cultures - from the Sumerian *Epic of Gilgamesh* to the Hindu *Ramayana*, from Dante's journey to the underworld in *The Divine Comedy* to the Persian poet, Farid ud-Din Attar's 'The Conference of the Birds', and Bunyan's *Pilgrim's Progress*. Reinvented in every age, the story appears in modern literature in *The Wizard of Oz, Lord of the Rings, Atlas Shrugged, Journey to the East,*

Star Wars, Indiana Jones, Watership Down, The Lion King, Cold Mountain, and even the Harry Potter novels.

As we follow the journey of the hero and his friends in any of these myths and stories, we see that our personal story echoes the events and truths of these stories. We identify with the characters, all of whom are transformed by their experiences, as we ourselves seek to be healed from life's difficult events. By participating in their experiences, we expand our own perceptions and understanding, and are able to feel renewed and enthused about life's possibilities.

The story of the search for the Holy Grail is also the journey of a hero, and the idea of transformation and healing is key to understanding it. It is part of the cycle of Arthurian legends first appearing in the work of the medieval French poet, Chretien de Troyes. It is reminiscent of some of the paradise myths already mentioned which deal with those who stumble upon hidden valleys. The Grail is a magical cup or bowl, said to have been used by Jesus at the Last Supper. As a young man, Perceval sees the Grail when he is in the mysterious Grail castle, where the Fisher King lies wounded, and his surrounding lands lie infertile and desolate. Perceval does not understand the power and significance of the Grail, and, overwhelmed by the splendour of the castle, fails to ask the important question – 'Whom does the Grail serve?' The Fisher King is unable to drink from the Grail and is therefore not healed. Perceval is given a sword to accomplish the tasks that lie ahead, but when he awakes the next morning, he is alone and there is no castle. He then spends the next twenty years trying to find the castle, with many a misadventure, but through which he proves himself worthy of returning to the castle.

The quest for the Holy Grail – the source of physical and spiritual sustenance - is very much a myth for our times, not least because our world too is becoming like the world of the Fisher King – a wasteland with rivers and lakes drying up, forests disappearing and the very body of the earth blasted and raped for its riches.

Most of us experience in youth a glimmer of something that seems extraordinary, even magical, when anything seems possible and the whole world glows. Just as quickly as this glimpse came, it disappears, but it can haunt us or so profoundly affect us that we spend the rest of our lives searching for it. Mistakenly we pursue our own personal happiness, exploring and experimenting with the external things of life, but the meaning of life is not to be found in external things and we find ourselves having to come to terms with suffering, dukka or 'unsatisfactoriness', as the

Buddha described it. It is each and every individual's task to understand that the meaning of life lies in the service of that which is greater than oneself.

In psychological terms, the ego has to be transcended, and the inner and outer worlds reconciled. In that reconciliation rests the hope for our world. Like Pandora's box, in Greek mythology, which once opened releases all the evils known to man – only one thing remains in the box after she has done the unthinkable – and that is hope. Hope we always need, and we never needed it more than now.

Myths therefore are relevant to how we live our lives. They help us understand that beneath the chaos, there is the possibility of redemption. All the great myths have the power to help us shift our perspective and change our lives. Reflecting on our values, motives and beliefs, we can make changes and move forward. Hope for the future is to be found in renewal and transformation. We have to begin with ourselves, but collectively we can work together to change the world for the better. Some individuals have already woken up to what needs to be done. Others prefer to remain as yet asleep, oblivious to the huge transition that is taking place in our world. But it is significant minorities that have changed history, and new ideas, as we shall see in the next chapter, are already taking root and beginning to transform our consciousness.

CHAPTER 3
Shift – the tipping point for conscious evolution

Given the crises we face, it seems that we have to change the way we live if we as a species, and other species on the planet, are to survive. Geologists and palaeontologists have been able to show that there have been five previous extinctions since the beginnings of life on earth. However, it has been species, not the planet itself, that were virtually wiped out and new forms of life emerged. So the real crisis is for us now – we, as the most advanced of all species, are the problem and it is we who have to learn to adapt if we are not to be extinguished. And adapt we can – we have the wit, we just need the intention. Rather than fearing that we will destroy ourselves, or naively trusting that everything will just get better and better, and we will live in some kind of paradise, a more realistic way of looking at the crises surrounding us are as the triggers for change. We may well be at the tipping point, the moment when change becomes unstoppable. Could evolution be unfolding in such a manner that we are maturing as a species and moving towards a higher order of being?

If we look at the history of the universe and the evolution

of life on earth, it is a truly amazing story. The latest ideas of western science with regard to evolution do not seem so unlike what ancient civilizations portrayed in myth, for example, the idea that many creation myths start with the world as a whole as in the cosmic egg myths, and then there is division, or the idea that the world was danced into existence as with the Greek myth of Gaia or the Hindu myth of Shiva and Shakti.

Cosmologists agree that before the appearance of matter the universe was an entangled matrix of invisible energy – 'the field'. After the Big Bang 13.7 billion years ago, physical matter precipitated out of that energy field although it is still entangled with it. The universe evolved from this state of pure energy which was hot and dense, then expanded and cooled repeatedly over billions of years until galaxies and stars were formed. Many kinds of atoms were created from particles within the stars, and when the earth cooled to a temperature that enabled life to begin, atoms combined with each other to form simple molecules. These molecules, existing in the rock dust, mud and water, evolved into larger molecules with the warmth of the sun and storm and earthquake activity. These larger molecules included proteins, amino acids, as well as RNA and DNA, which enabled them gradually to join together, working to copy and build a system that meant they could multiply by reproducing themselves. As more molecules joined together, simple cells were created.

These simple cells (around three and a half billion years ago) were bacteria. As they multiplied and divided into different strains, the first major crisis occurred – there was insufficient food for them all in the form of gases, minerals and organic molecules. So they discovered a new way of feeding themselves by trapping sunlight and turning it into energy – photosynthesis. Unfortunately a side effect of this was that over time photosynthesis produced another crisis for the bacteria – a poisonous waste gas which was dangerous to them – oxygen. And as if that wasn't bad enough, yet another danger threatened them in the form of ultra-violet light which was building up and threatening to fry them. However, the extra oxygen combined to form a layer of ozone in the upper layer of the atmosphere which prevented the ultra-violet light from reaching them. As more oxygen built up, enzymes were produced by some of the bacteria which rendered the oxygen harmless. Later on, other bacteria evolved which were able to use the oxygen to extract more energy from their food, and ultimately went on to become animals, whilst the bacteria who still obtained their food via photosynthesis evolved into plants.

So these early life forms were inventive in the face of crises, finding new ways of dealing with problems and evolving new lifestyles. Under pressure, when danger threatens, it seems that life becomes extraordinarily inventive. The crises seem to have driven evolution, with new forms of life emerging in response to environmental upheaval. The adaptation and evolution seems to have been one of ever-increasing complexity and diversity, and most importantly communicative and co-operative, and we shall see this intensified with the next stages of evolution.

Once oxygen had stabilized at a concentration of 21% of the earth's atmosphere, the larger bacteria which were still single-celled joined together in co-operative groups with a nucleus, in which the genetic material was encapsulated. Two cells were now able to come together and through sexual reproduction produce offspring that contained a combination of their genetic materials. This enabled yet more adaptations. Increasing numbers meant increasing competition for food, but the response to this was single cells joining together, with different cells taking on different functions for greater efficiency. It does not seem to have been a question of the fittest driving evolution, but rather 'co-operation, interaction and mutual dependence', as the biologist Lynn Margulis has shown.

Greater complexity always seems to have resulted in yet more complex organisms, but each time competition resulted in co-operation becoming the means whereby life forms evolved. This increased co-operation resulted in greater evolutionary success because organisms became more efficient and effective. It also seems as if the same systems were being used over and over again in ever more complex arrangements. Fractals (from the Latin fractus meaning broken or fractured) seem to be part of the fundamental physics of nature, whereby rough or fragmented geometric shapes can be split into parts, each of which is similar to the whole.

As organisms developed, the nervous system, organs and brain developed with rapid communication between different parts of the body, allowing more flexible behaviour. Within vertebrates the spine developed with the main nerve centres at the top becoming the first simple brains. Human brains have evolved and grown from early homo erectus (about 1.7 million years ago), developing the cortex and more recently the neo-cortex. With the emergence of self-reflective consciousness, humans became unique amongst species in having the freedom to decide behaviour and a need to make sense of the world.

If over millions of years, and indeed several extinctions when countless species were wiped out, life continued to evolve by adapting and mutating as a response to crises, is it possible that we as a species are still evolving? Could it be that in response to the challenges we now face, we might be about to take our next leap forward in evolution? Evolution always goes beyond what went before, transcending and including, and increasing its depth. Could a new kind of human being evolve, perhaps one that is more conscious and aware, a more mature and caring one? Cynics may well mock this idea as a naive hope, but it is the nature of cynicism not to be open to ideas that challenge the status quo. Galileo after all was condemned as a heretic in the seventeenth century because he challenged the then prevailing geocentric view that the earth was the centre of the universe, not the sun. As the philosopher Schopenhauer said when talking of truth, 'first it is ridiculed, second it is violently opposed, third it is accepted as self-evident.'

In spite of our indisputable ability to have made the most amazing advances in science, medicine and technology, and to live, at least in many parts of the world, in some considerable comfort and luxury, we know this has been at great cost to others in the world and to the planet itself. The problem is that we see ourselves as separate from nature and from each other. As human beings we don't seem to have evolved very much at all. We're driven by self-interest, and don't equate our needs and desires with any negative impact on the rest of humanity or other species, because we fail to see ourselves as part of an interrelated whole.

But human beings have not always seen themselves as separate from nature and from each other. It is clear that an organic worldview once prevailed (and amongst indigenous people still exists to some extent), as we saw in chapter 2, where men and women were intimately linked with the world around them. By the 6th century BCE and the time of the ancient Greek civilization there was a split between one school of thought that held that nature was alive, with everything forming and reforming in an endless process of making order out of chaos, and another school of thought that held that the world was a rigidly perfect, mechanical one, without purpose. Over time it became expedient for this latter view of a mechanized world to be seen as being created by a single, all-powerful God and it was this view that came to prevail in the West.

The influence of Descartes, Bacon and Newton meant that the mechanistic-reductionist worldview of separateness, that sees nature as something that must be controlled, was reinforced by Darwin's theory of evolution, which sees humanity as an evolutionary accident, where only the fittest survive. And today, the logical deduction that has been made from this approach is that there is no need for God. But in evicting God, meaning has been lost from life, and such a worldview has resulted in the kind of society we have constructed for ourselves and is responsible for many of our ills.

Something other than chance surely has to be responsible for our world. Pioneers of the new science have challenged many of the laws of biology and physics, such as Rupert Sheldrake with his theory of morphogenetic fields and the concept of collective memory, or Karl Pribram with his work on the holographic brain, or Jacques Benveniste with his idea of the memory of water and the ability of molecules to vibrate and communicate, or Dean Radin with his concept of group coherence and a collective global mind. The ideas of these pioneers, often scorned by the establishment, challenge our current view of how the world works, and seem to affirm the idea of a life-force flowing through the universe. The life-force, or matrix of all form, or zero-point energy field seems to equate with the idea of the universal consciousness, God, the Secret Force, or to use terms from eastern philosophy – Brahman, Dharmakaya or the Tao. As the author Lynne McTaggart says in her book, *The Field: The Quest for the Secret Force of the Universe*, 'Human beings and all living things are a coalescence of energy connected to every other thing in the world. This pulsating energy field is the central engine of our being and our consciousness, the alpha and the omega of our existence.'

The eastern worldview has tended to be very different from that which has dominated western civilization. It is dynamic, alive, organic. The underlying elements are the same, regardless of historical, geographical or cultural differences. At the heart of the eastern worldview is the awareness of the unity and interrelationship of the interdependent parts of a cosmic whole. There is one ultimate, indivisible reality. In our western worldview we divide the world into separate objects and events, with the natural world being seen as composed of separate parts to be controlled and exploited by us for our benefit. We ourselves are also split – the mind is separate from the body. This may help us cope with everyday life, but it is not reality, and has alienated us from our fellow human beings and from nature itself. It's as if we're participating in a collective hallucination!

In reality we're all interdependent cells within the great super-organism that is the planet. James Lovelock's Gaia

Theory, which had its roots in the ideas of James Hutton, the father of geology, was once scoffed at but is now more widely accepted. Lovelock maintains that the world is a living entity with its own consciousness, a single self-regulating organism. Gaia, our earth, has the capacity to maintain a balance through *homeostasis* (Greek, meaning to keep the same), and to modify the temperature, the atmosphere, the salinity and pH of the oceans etc. in order for life to continue. We can draw a parallel with how our own body works to sustain life. Each of us comprises trillions of cells, all living and working in harmony to maintain a balance. The cells co-operate and the organs work together in functions such as breathing, feeding, eliminating etc., not in competition with each other. In the same way as our cells and organs are part of the whole that is each of us, so we are living beings within a larger being. Communities of organisms work together, each maintaining its own identity while contributing to the life of the whole, each balancing its own needs with the needs of the larger community. Similarly, we need to work together, co-operating, not competing, with each other, and adapting and modifying our behaviour so that we can deal with the crises our civilization is experiencing.

But how do we adopt a more co-operative approach to functioning in the world when for so long a worldview has prevailed that means we behave in a way that puts our own way of life first, with no real thought for other people or species, or for the processes of nature which are so finely balanced? We can only solve this conundrum by becoming more fully conscious human beings. The crises are clarion calls to see the necessity for changing ourselves and our behaviour. Until we do that there is no real hope of changing anything else in the world, and there is the risk that unless we adapt and change pretty fast, we may be too late to save our species.

However, the good news is that the revolution in awareness is already underway as a growing number of people worldwide commit themselves to a different approach to life, and the numbers are growing exponentially. There has been a movement for many decades now for an alternative, more holistic, environmentally responsible, more compassionate lifestyle. The sociologist Paul Ray has termed people who adopt such a lifestyle 'cultural creatives'. This subculture has grown out of the environmental, human rights and consciousness movements from the 1960s onwards.

When new values which are more balanced and more compassionate are adopted, there is a tendency to act more in the interest of the whole than one's own self-interest. Technology can be used more wisely and with appropriate humility and respect for nature. It's not a question of reverting to an earlier stage of existence. That would be pointless for humanity in its life on earth so far has accomplished a great deal whether we look at the provision of security, food, housing and freedom for many, or the spread of universal principles of law and democracy, or positive and liberating achievements like education and international commerce, with all the benefits they bring. The imperative now is for us once again to function in harmony with the living world. We need to re-find the connection that ancient civilizations possessed and that has never been lost by indigenous peoples like the Native Americans or the Aborigines, for example, in which the earthly environment is seen as a whole entity and the role of spirit is paramount. That was of course the original purpose of religion. The Latin word *religare*, from which 'religion' is derived, means to bind together - the individual with society, the world and the cosmos.

We can look at the chaos in our world and feel despair as disintegration threatens to overwhelm us, but as things become ever more complex, maybe it's not a total collapse of civilization that we're facing, but breakthrough to a new and very different kind of existence. In the world of quantum physics the universe is now seen as a dynamic, constantly changing web of interrelationships, with atoms and particles whirling around, not fixed and solid. Chaos theory shows that the evolution of complex systems always involves alternating periods of order and chaos. It seems that once a point of chaos is reached, out of the blue something appears to drive evolution in one direction or another.

Ilya Prigogine, the physicist and chemical engineer who won the Nobel Prize for chemistry in 1977 for his pioneering work on 'dissipative structures', demonstrated how living systems, even at the experimental level, can recreate new order when they reach a state of chaos. Structures that are breaking down, whatever they may be, recreate themselves into a new pattern. The extreme fluctuations, or crises, result in new levels of organization emerging from the chaos. So if our civilization increasingly appears chaotic and at breaking point, a breakthrough could well be on the cards. Could it be that our next evolutionary leap is about to happen? Maybe the crises are the catalysts which will push us, if we adapt successfully, to a new and higher level of evolution.

Way back last century the visionary French Jesuit priest, palaeontologist, biologist and philosopher, Teilhard de Chardin, spent much of his life studying fossils and the natural world and trying to integrate religious experience with natural science, and in particular, Christian theology with theories of evolution. He saw evidence of a larger, spiritual world underlying and giving birth to the materal which would then transform itself. He envisaged what he called the 'Omega point' – a kind of endpoint of evolution, or the divine destiny of evolution, by which the universe was moving towards a maximum level of consciousness resulting in a new state of peace and planetary unity. The idea has been taken up by many, including the mathematical physicist and cosmologist, Frank J. Tippler. He sees it as the ultimate fate of the universe as required by the laws of physics (not that everyone agrees with him, needless to say). The idea has also permeated popular culture from science fiction writers like Isaac Asimov, or Arthur C. Clarke to the best-selling author Dan Brown.

Teilhard de Chardin talked of the geosphere, the hydrosphere and the biosphere but he also suggested that the earth was growing a new organ of consciousness called the 'noosphere' (from the Greek *noos*, meaning mind), the mind-sphere, analogous on a planetary level to the evolution of the cerebral cortex in humans. The cerebral cortex is the most highly developed part of the brain, where most of the information processing takes place, and plays a key role in perception, attention, awareness, memory, thought, language and consciousness. It is also the most recent structure in terms of brain evolution.

According to Teilhard de Chardin, the 'noosphere' is a planetary thinking network – an interlinked system of consciousness and information, a global net of self-awareness, instantaneous feedback and communication. He regarded humanity as moving towards being a single group able to think as one consciousness. Similar ideas were also held by Sri Aurobindo, the influential Bengali philosopher and mystic. He saw man as a 'transitional being', able to transcend human nature but also able to transform it, living in the world with an evolved consciousness. He saw evolution as progressing towards a 'Supermind', a complete all-embracing consciousness.

The fascinating thing about all this is that both men wrote about this long before computers, the internet and all the technological advances we take for granted today had been invented. Now 5 billion people have mobiles and 2 billion subscribe to the Internet, there are over 100 million dot coms and new communities of individuals who only know each other through the Cloud (remote server computers) and can become digital nomads living and working anywhere in the world. Technology now links us in ways we never imagined – a veritable web of interconnected minds, a global nervous system. The web has shrunk the world, and now anyone can communicate his/her message to anyone else, with the potential to transform the world. 800 million people now use Facebook, which has a target of 1 billion users by 2012, with the biggest growth to come in Asia and South America. There are also a growing number of more niche networks, for example, LinkedIn for professionals, ResearchGate for scientists, or Ravelry for knitting and crochet enthusiasts if that's your thing.

Facebook and Twitter can report as events happen in one part of the world, with an instant reaction that can influence those same events as they unfold, as we saw most vividly in the Arab Spring. Never before have we had such tools at our disposal, and whilst they present the most amazing opportunity for a worldwide exchange of information and ideas, they also present dangers, as can be seen with criminal and terrorist exploitation of the Internet. I'm reminded at this point of the Chinese character for crisis, wei-chi, which consists of two halves, one representing opportunity for change, the other, danger.

It really does seem as if the planet could be developing a kind of global brain. Various people have written about the concept of some kind of world, or planetary or global brain, from H.G. Wells in 1937 to more recent

authors like Peter Russell, Howard Bloom and Joel de
Rosnay. Peter Russell's work particularly interests me,
because he emphasizes the need for communication
technologies to be linked with spiritual technologies
like yoga and meditation. Peter Russell studied maths,
theoretical physics and computer science and psychology
at Cambridge University. He also studied Transcendental
Meditation with the Maharishi and conducted research into
the psychology of meditation at the University of Bristol.
In 1983 when his book *The Global Brain* was first published
it was before the current explosion of technology and
seemed ahead of its time. Events have proved the author
to be spot on. He maintains that we have now reached a
crossroads in evolution, with the internet linking humanity
into one world-wide community, with billions of cells in
the brain being able to communicate with every other cell.
Communication technology has increased dramatically in
both speed and complexity, enabling humanity to become
potentially a social super-organism of independent
wholes. Rather more than just bees in a hive, or ants in a
colony, or flocks of birds, who can communicate as super-
organisms, we humans could grow together mentally with
linked minds, interacting with all the other minds within
the social super-organism, bringing us to a new level of
evolution. Just as the electrical and chemical activities of
many separate nerve cells in our brain give rise to a single

integrated consciousness in us, so the internet could be the mechanism which enables billions of cells to communicate with every other cell of a giant global brain. This in turn might just produce a more conscious planet.

Recently scientists have uploaded information into a monkey's brain via a wire and tiny electrodes in what is thought to be the first transmission of electronic data direct into a primate brain. Although this is part of a project aimed at helping people with paralysis to become more mobile (the Walk Again Project at Duke University, North Carolina), this breakthrough could have wider implications, eventually allowing humans to control computers and machines by thought alone, and perhaps even to communicate with each other. Technology is moving so fast that it may well not be long before direct social networking could happen with friends, family and work colleagues via a brain net. Intel, Google and Microsoft have already created their own divisions to work on such ideas.

According to Michio Kaku, theoretical physicist and popularizer of science, computer chips will be everywhere in the future, not just in our appliances, but in our clothes too. Then there are incredible materials being developed like Graphene, a super-strong, super-light natural substance derived from graphite. Medical scientists wants to utilize it to make tiny devices for diagnosis and treatment, food packagers want to use it to keep foods fresher for longer, and bicycle and aircraft manufacturers want to employ it because of its incredible lightness. We could be talking about developments like touch-screen devices that can be rolled up or folded away, and it might even enable the production of cheaper electricity via photovoltaic cells. Steve Fuller, Chair in Social Epistemology at Warwick University's Department of Sociology, feels that science has always been enhancing the human condition, making the world more accessible and usable by us, whether we're talking about the development of agriculture or computers amplifying and extending our capabilities. High tech companies like Google, IBM and Hewlett Packard are now planning ultra-miniaturized computers little larger than a speck of dust – 'smart dust', which will be installed underground, in household appliances and inside clothes, all connected through world-wide networks.

We will soon be able to re-engineer our own body parts and because of cell repair live well beyond 150 years. Aubrey de Grey, biomedical gerontologist and Chief Science officer of SENS (Strategies for Engineered Negligible Senescence), says: 'We are seeing the emergence of a new era of medicine where the diseases of ageing can be blocked or even reversed. These therapies are mostly in research now but eventually they will be commonplace.'

Robots are becoming increasingly sophisticated and artificial intelligence is making great strides.
The Hatfield Project at the University of Hertfordshire, for example, is part of a series of trials involving scientists in Japan, the US and Britain who are developing robots and AI. Robots have been used commercially and industrially for many years now, but humanoid robots are a new development, with human-like appearance and behaviour. Bina48 (part of the LifeNaut project) is reputed to be the best the world currently has. Built by robotics guru, David Hanson, in Vermont, Bina48 has a very human appearance. Made out of Frubber which gives the appearance of human flesh and skin, while 30 motors replicate human expression and head movements, Bina48 is able to recognize speech and to answer. A one-off prototype, it may well be a harbinger of things to come, a computer so lifelike and responsive it will be hard to tell it apart from a human being. The Japanese firm Kokoro, together with Professor Hiroshi Ishiguro at Osaka University, has created 'Geminoid DK', another realistic robot, with the express aim of studying human-robot interaction. They are also behind the fembot, 'Yume'.

Boston Dynamics is part of a £17million project for the US army. Still a long way from taking over from humans on the battlefield, Petman is being used to test protective qualities of chemical warfare suits for combat soldiers. Two robotic quadrupeds, called Alphadogs, are due to begin military testing in the field by US forces in 2012 and will carry up to 400lbs of kit across rough terrain.

We're also seeing the creation of machines that aren't necessarily trying to be humans but still interactive and to be emotionally intelligent companions, whether Sony's Aibo robotic dogs for children or ' Paro', a Japanese designed baby seal robot, to provide comfort and companionship for the elderly. 'Kaspar' is a robot designed to take into schools where autistic children are taught. Research is going on into how teams of robots might be able to interact with people safely and comfortably, helping with simple tasks like fetching and carrying, controlling TVs and stereos, prompting on medication which could be of great assistance with the sick and elderly.

Then there's the Watson robot, an IBM designed talking supercomputer. Watson is able to store 200 million pages of data, including dictionaries and encyclopaedias, and takes only 3 seconds to review the database. There are hopes that Watson's technologies will help with all kinds of tasks from diagnosing diseases more quickly and accurately to helping solve traffic problems and assisting with corporate strategic decisions and predicting risk and market change.

Whereas some may fear that robots, androids and cyborgs might run amok, as portrayed in movie series like Star Wars and Terminator, Ray Kurzweil, a leading authority on AI as well as influential futurist and successful engineer and inventor, takes a much more positive view – 'it's not an alien invasion...We're creating them to make ourselves smarter.' In the not-too-distant future he believes that computers will be more intelligent than humans. When that happens (around 2045 Kurzweil believes) then humanity will be transformed. He calls this 'the Singularity', after a term in astrophysics meaning a point in space-time at which the rules of ordinary physics do not apply. Biotechnology and nanotechnology will enable us to manipulate our bodies and the world around us – at the molecular level. Evolution can then happen by 'intelligent direction'. Kurzweil might be regarded as extreme, but The Brain Mind Institute in Lausanne, Switzerland, is working on a neuron-by-neuron simulation of a mammalian brain on an IBM computer. The hope is that it will be possible to simulate a human brain within the next 10 years.

There is no denying that amidst all the extraordinary

technological developments that are increasing exponentially, we have incredible potential for the next stage of evolution. We are in a transition period at present, fraught with crises and upheaval, but these could be the triggers, just as at an earlier stage of evolution the oxygen and the food crises and the extinctions were triggers for evolutionary progress. Potential catastrophe could still be averted, for clearly we have the means of shaping our own future. However, although the external shifts and upheavals are taking place, we also have to make an inner shift. We do not have to keep repeating the patterns of the past. Each of us has to make a fundamental change to our thinking by altering our perceptions about the way we think the world is. Only then can we embark on a path of personal transformation and join with others who are also on that path to change the course of evolutionary history and awaken consciousness, enabling the 'empathizing of the planet'.

The mind is much deeper than we realize. On the surface, we're aware of our conscious feelings and thoughts which flood our mind during the course of our daily life. But we are not primarily the products of our conscious thinking but rather the products of the thinking that is going on below the level of awareness. Most of our decisions are based on prejudice and emotion – we are not the logical thinkers we tend to believe we are. Our perceptions are subconscious beliefs that we have unwittingly acquired and are ingrained in us at a cellular level. We acquire them during the earliest years of our lives from our parents, friends, teachers and the media and they have a tremendous influence on the way we see ourselves even though we're not normally aware of them. They can often be limiting and self-sabotaging and responsible for much of our need to reaffirm and bolster our sense of identity. They can affect us in everything we do in our lives unless we try consciously to change them. Candace Pert, a renowned neuroscientist and pharmacologist, proved through her experiments that we perceive through this filter of subconscious beliefs, ignoring more than 90 per cent of available information. Our minds and thoughts shape our world. The revolution in consciousness understanding in recent years has helped us see more clearly how we are ruled more by the unconscious mind than the rational mind. Most of our decisions are based on prejudice and emotion – we are not the logical thinkers we tend to believe we are. The Institute of Heart Math, since it was set up in 1991, has done a huge amount of research on stress and how the heart responds to emotional and mental reactions. Learning to shift out of stressful emotional states into more positive perceptions and emotions is enormously beneficial.

Beneath the subconscious level of our mind however is a far deeper level - the superconscious. At this level we are part of a greater whole – the infinite field of consciousness, the Zero Point Field, the Holy Spirit, the Self, or whatever name is given to it by various religious traditions. It is eternal and pervades everything and can be accessed through meditation, yoga, prayer and healing, or sometimes through shock or near-death experience. The rishis, or seers, of ancient India, the great teachers of the Axial Age (beginning around 600 BCE) who gave birth to an extraordinary flowering of religious and philosophical traditions from Buddha and Confucius to Socrates and Plato, and all mystics throughout the ages have accessed such spiritual technology.

We too can all have access to it to change our programmed beliefs. Utilized on a regular basis we come to truly know ourselves, by understanding the nature of mind. The great analytical psychologist, Carl Jung, believed that an epochal shift was taking place in the contemporary psyche. In his view, the more we come to know ourselves, the more in touch we will be with the collective consciousness, and the less we will be driven by the desires and fears of the ego which limit us as human beings.

Bruce Lipton, the cell biologist, believes that we can change the perceptions that prevent us from experiencing ourselves at this deeper level. He argues that we can physically change the cell membranes of our bodies because they respond to our thoughts. He believes that the cell membrane is the equivalent of each cell's brain, functioning as the active intelligence of the cell. Interacting with cell membranes enables us to change our lives, health and even our genes. We have the power to control our biology and to become masters of our fate, not its victims.

Working with leading physicists from the University of Arizona, Princeton University, the international Institute of Biophysics, Cambridge University and the Institute of Noetic Sciences, Lynne McTaggart's experiments have shown how our thoughts and intentions can affect and change the world. It is not a huge leap to see that our intentions will be reflected in the unfolding of evolution itself.

Over billions of years bacteria evolved and flourished, as we have seen, because they were able to adapt and mutate, with the surviving organisms actually changing their genetics. Evolution came about through organisms joining together in co-operation, forming super-organisms. Just as in the human body cells and organs work together enabling the whole to function, so humans can work together to enable the body of the planet to function. Quantum physics has proved how information processed by our minds influences the way we see the world (the so-called observer effect), so since our minds actively co-create the world we experience, by changing our perceptions we have an opportunity to change our world. We can reprogramme ourselves by using psychological techniques like neurolinguistic programming (NLP) or cognitive behavioural therapy (CBT), through meditation, prayer and cultivating feelings of compassion for others, and in doing this we become conscious participants in our own evolution. With a positive, healing vision of our world's future we can ensure that we break through to the next level of evolution.

PART II
The Age of Wisdom: Transforming our World

CHAPTER 4
Conscious community - cultivating well-being and happiness

Human beings have always joined together in society to achieve what they were unable to accomplish on their own – from the very earliest hunter-gatherer tribes of the Stone Age, to the simple horticultural lifestyle of the Neolithic cultures, and then the agricultural based societies, to fortified towns and cities, and ultimately states and empires, with ever more complex social organization. Earliest societies seem to have been peaceful, egalitarian, sharing land and other resources and not making war (see chapter 3). Around 4000 BCE there seems to have been a huge change in culture due to climate change and desertification, causing mass migration that resulted in violent invasion by migrating hordes. Since then we've had endless wars, male domination, oppression and inequality. Recently however there seems to be a recognition that even though this continues, the world is slowly getting better.

During the Industrial and Post-industrial Age a wealth- and power-oriented culture has been dominant as a result of the prevailing individualistic consciousness where we've come to see ourselves as separate from nature and from other human beings, and looking out for ourselves and nearest and dearest only. This has been disastrous in terms of our collective behaviour where we have seen no wrong in exploiting our fellow human-beings one way or another and taking from the earth more than we needed, resulting in our current crises. Although progress and prosperity have brought many benefits to the Western world, the cost in terms of worldwide human suffering and the environment is only now beginning to dawn on us. An open society has allowed us considerable freedom, but we have not always used that freedom wisely. We seem to lack the wisdom that many of those indigenous tribal societies still in existence (though rapidly vanishing) appear to have retained where living in community and in harmony with the natural world is paramount. Much of their deep ecological wisdom is based on centuries of observation of the natural world. To indigenous peoples (just as with the early hunter-gatherer societies) all natural things are alive, imbued with the spirit-force that flows through them. There is then no question of destroying the environment – in fact they are taught to think of the good of the whole above the needs of the individual and to consider the consequences of their actions for the generations to come.

However, it is possible that we are entering a new

historical phase. Over the last two hundred years, in spite of two World Wars in the twentieth century and the murder of millions of people by Stalin, Hitler, Pol Pot and others, we still may be becoming progressively less violent, and there has been progress in terms of attitudes changing, at least in the West. According to Steven Pinker, Professor of Psychology at Harvard, both murder and warfare have declined. Brutality, barbarism and cruelty are not on the scale they once were, though they still continue. From the second half of the eighteenth century we have seen improvement in social conditions – the end of the slave trade, a new concept of democracy with the American Revolution and Declaration of Independence, the emancipation of women, the rise of socialism, changing attitudes to gender and the body, more empathy for the natural world and for indigenous peoples. And maybe it's just a question of time before the horrors that we see on our TV screens are finally confined to history. Is it possible that we are now at a point where, faced with crises that seem insurmountable, we can begin to see ourselves not as separate from nature but as part of a giant whole, a superorganism (see chapter 3)? Without advocating a return to more primitive times, could it be that we can move forward to having a more mature understanding of what being part of society really means and change our behaviour accordingly? And is it possible that we could speed up the process of evolution in time to save humanity from destroying itself?

Let's consider for a moment the nature of human development, which doesn't stop at adulthood but continues throughout life. Being an infant, becoming a child, an adolescent and then maturing into an adult are transitory stages in human development. Maturation means further growth, developing resilience, fulfilling our potential as human beings and becoming wiser in the process. It's about flourishing and becoming empathic, ie. being able to think of others and how best we can contribute to their well-being as well as our own.

Society matures in the same way. At present we're in transition from a society that is really still in adolescence and trying to move into adulthood. As adolescents we are driven by ego, but we seem to be displaying the worst excesses of any spoilt, self-obsessed adolescent, having an over-developed sense of ego, resulting in greed, aggression, exploitation, winning at all costs – the very behaviours which have caused the dilemmas we now face. Just as a truly mature adult behaves differently from an adolescent, so too does a society which is becoming more mature and rich in wisdom. It has a totally different sense of purpose, thinking of the whole rather than one's own self-interest.

Elizabet Sahtouris has shown how in evolution ancient bacteria evolved into single-celled organisms which evolved into multi-celled creatures and then colonies (see chapter 3). As life evolved on the planet, solutions for problems were found by parts of the whole finding a balance. Creatures seem to have changed themselves in response to environmental stresses and through co-operating. All creatures and environments co-evolve by changing themselves and one another. Some creatures took to dry land and continued to evolve there, until, relatively late in the history of the planet, humans began to organize themselves into communities in much the same way as the ancient bacteria had.

So how might today's society become more mature, more caring, and fairer for all? This is not something that governments can legislate for, though it can help in the process by contributing to changing the culture. It seems that the rights of the individual and the interests of the whole have to be balanced. The challenge is to spread the understanding of how interrelated everything is. When we humans see ourselves as part of a greater whole, one part of a much greater living system, then fundamental change can take place in the way we think and behave. Whereas the old worldview that has dominated our society for the last three hundred years sees us as separate from each other and from nature, the worldview of the mature society recognizes that everything is interdependent and that the good of the whole society and the environment is of paramount importance.

As we face up to the problems we have in both our own Western society and the rest of the world, we're beginning to understand that our own personal happiness and peace of mind are not something separate from what is going on elsewhere on the planet. We can see that we are connected to each other – we always have been but modern technology makes this more apparent than ever before. So long as there is suffering somewhere else in the world, we are affected. And if our way of life has a negative impact on others and the ecology of the world we inhabit, then we need to rethink our approach to life – we all have a shared interest in transformation. We have to create a future that works for everyone, all life forms, as well as future generations. Nothing less than a new culture is required - one that is based on wisdom. No longer can we manipulate the environment as we have done, or exploit others for our own ends and ignore those less fortunate than ourselves.

We need to transform our society into a more equal and compassionate one. We need a different vision of society where individuals have a sense of social responsibility and the contribution they can make to it, recognizing that co-operation is very powerful in terms of what it can achieve. The selfish society that we have become is no longer sustainable. And we're all guilty of this. It's not just bankers paying themselves fat bonuses, or chief executives getting eye-watering pay deals that are obscenely greater than their staff are paid, or politicians on the gravy train, or overrated celebrities capitalizing on their brand - we've all become more selfish in society. Research at the University of Michigan Institute for Social Research (Sara Konrath) has shown how even students are more selfish than they were two decades ago. Analysing surveys involving almost 14,000 college students over the past thirty years, 'Generation Me' was found to be too engrossed in their own lives to care about others. This is probably because, as British psychoanalytic psychotherapist, Sue Gerhardt argues in her book *The Selfish Society: How we all forgot to love one another and made money instead*, recent generations of children have not been brought up to consider others and always put themselves first, largely because they have been starved of attention in their formative years, though they may well have been provided with plenty of toys and gadgets. The 2011 UNICEF Report on child wellbeing in the UK, Spain and Sweden shows how children want to spend time with family and friends, nurtured by attention and shared activities rather than having lots of material possessions.

There has been significant social change with regard to the family in the last few decades: both parents working or the sole parent in a single family working; mothers returning to work soon after a child's birth; and nursery care increasingly taking the place of parental care. Feminism has been blamed by some for this, but feminism freed women to make appropriate choices for themselves. Many working mothers have found fulfilment in their careers at the same time as bringing up children who are happy and successful themselves. Rather more significant as a contributing factor to the problem has been the effect consumerism has had, with material wellbeing seen as the most important objective in life. An obsession with celebrity, reality TV and the 'bling' culture have exacerbated the problem.

Over the last three decades the rich have got richer and the super rich richer than ever, although there has not been a social group that has not benefited from increased material wealth in the West to some degree. We have focused on material living standards and economic growth as our major priority, while the inequality gap between the rich and the poor has grown ever wider. This is in spite of large sums of money having been directed towards low-income families.

In his study of great civilizations that collapsed, *A Study of History*, Arnold Toynbee identified two major reasons for the demise of those civilizations: first, the concentration of wealth in the hands of the few; second, inflexibility under stress. In their book, *The Spirit Level*, Richard Wilkinson and Kate Pickett show how social problems and crime get worse when the differential between rich and poor is too great. They came to this conclusion after charting levels of crime, stress, drug and alcohol abuse, obesity and depression across 20 of the world's richest countries, and although they have their critics, their findings seem to ring true.

We have the vast gap between rich and poor, and our society is showing all the signs of breakdown. All developed countries are finding that the structure of society is now very different from what it was some decades ago, with the decline of extended families, more single people, unemployment, immigration, and an increasingly ageing population – ie. a far greater number of dependent people. Financial hardship, homelessness, and crime tend to be the consequence, exacerbated by the tough economic climate that prevails. By contrast, the excesses of the mega-rich seem obscene, even though some donate a great deal of money to charity and the arts. Others play the system, putting properties into offshore companies, and employing advisers and accountants to help them avoid paying tax. However, there is every reason to hope that this will change. Inequality is now a subject of huge debate, and there is a general recognition that we need to address society's problems. Fixed ideas cannot any longer be held on to when the whole fabric of society is showing signs of stress.

Perhaps our current crises demonstrate that the days of never-ending material growth and consumption and debt are gone forever. The effect on the environment of unrestrained growth, using up materials and resources with no thought for the future, is something which people are becoming increasingly aware of. We have in any case been chasing rainbows, for material wealth has not brought happiness to those societies that have made it their priority. Affluence has increased significantly since the 1950s but we are no happier as a society than we were then. As the psychologist David Myers put it so well in his essay, 'What is the good life?' (on American society, but equally applicable to all of Western society):

'...big houses and broken homes, high incomes and low morale, secured rights and diminished civility. We were excelling at making a living but too often failing at making a life. We celebrated our prosperity but yearned for purpose. We cherished our freedoms but longed for connection. In an age of plenty, we were feeling spiritual hunger. These facts of life lead us to a startling conclusion: our becoming better off materially has not made us better off psychologically.'

The correlation between wealth and happiness doesn't work, because it's human nature to compare ourselves with others. Way back in 1896 Thorstein Veblen coined the term 'conspicuous consumption' in his book, *The Theory of The Leisure Class*, and argued that people seek status through consumption of luxuries which made their owners feel wealthy, but the problem was that everyone else aspired to have the same. And once everyone has the same thing, after a while no one is any happier. Conspicuous consumption can only provide short-lived pleasure, and modern media and advertising tend to encourage competitive appetites for luxury goods, an appetite that is insatiable for those who have the wherewithal, and for those that haven't there is only envy and a sense of failure.

It's true that money can't buy us happiness, although a certain amount to cover our basic needs is essential.

Once we have enough for those needs, there seems to be diminishing returns in the happiness stakes proportional to the increasing amount of money made, according to the Easterlin Paradox, a theory put forward in 1974 by Richard Easterlin (now Economics Professor at the University of Southern California). Not everyone agrees with this theory, although many governments across the world have used it to promote egalitarian policies. In spite of disagreement, economists have pointed out that unhappy people are bad for the economy and have suggested that we need to focus on measuring people's happiness rather than their income. Two Professors of Economics, Curtis Eaton and Mukesh Eswaran, have suggested that once a country reaches a reasonable standard of living, there is little further benefit to be had from increasing the wealth of the population. Indeed it could even make people worse off. As people seek to improve their status through competitive consumerism, working and shopping more, they have less time or inclination to help others, thus producing a more selfish society, where neighbourliness declines, community is damaged and trust disappears, with all the social consequences that we are now familiar with. Anxiety and depression seem to increase, along with alcoholism, drugs and crime.

As the economic climate has become tougher and the

spectre of rising unemployment adds to society's problems, so we are forced to reappraise the world and the values by which we live. People are now asking whether our materialistic society has somehow lost the ability to strive in a meaningful way.

A decade ago Paul Ray and Sherry Anderson's work on 'Cultural Creatives' revealed how our modern way of life has resulted in significant numbers of people seeking alternative ways of living, with the result that a more holistic society is now emerging in which ethical values and rebuilding community are seen as paramount. Cultural Creatives tend to be committed to personal growth and spirituality, they tend to use complementary medicine and buy organic food, as well as being involved in the peace movement, the human rights movement, NGOs etc. Dr Ray continues to explore what he now calls 'the emerging Wisdom Culture', which he believes is as significant as the Renaissance was 600 years ago in terms of a new values system evolving.

In their book, *Walk Out, Walk On: A Learning Journey into Communities Daring to Live the Future Now*, Margaret Wheatley and Deborah Freeze show how communities from Mexico to India to South Africa are rediscovering and recreating community. Around the world people have 'walked out' of familiar lives and 'walked on' to create healthy and resilient communities by working together in ground-breaking ways to create a new future. 'Walk Outs Who Walk On' are people who 'have walked out of a world of unsolved problems, scarce resources, limiting beliefs, and destructive individualism. They've walked on to beliefs and practices that solve problems and reveal abundant resources. They've created communities where everyone is welcome to learn, grow, and contribute. They've walked out of the greed and grasping of this time, where many individuals try to get as much as they can, and walked on to discover how to create what they need with what they have.'

The good news is that this is happening in thousands of places across the globe. A different world beyond consumerism and its insidious side effects is achievable. Through the power of community and self-organization, discovering the intelligence and inventiveness we all possess, solutions can be found to the problems we face and people can take control of the future. An amazing number of communities of all kinds now exist around the world, whether intentional communities, eco-villages, communes, ashrams, kibbutz, retreat centres or other co-operative living arrangements. Some of these have an educational aspect for visitors with workshops, conferences etc. and have now become very well known like Auroville in India, Findhorn in Scotland, or Damanhur in Italy.

Ultimately quality of life is what counts and that means achieving a work-life balance, improving psychological and social wellbeing, focusing on health, happiness, friendship, sharing, and community life.   In recent years psychologists and neuroscientists have increasingly been paying attention to what makes people happy. Whereas once exploring the pursuit of happiness was the realm of ivory-towered scholars, philosophers and religious teachers, a whole new science of positive psychology has now emerged. Psychology was until recently more interested in understanding what made people mentally ill or depressed, but now psychologists are exploring how, why and under what conditions individuals and communities can thrive. Using population surveys, and monitoring and measuring different levels of activity in different parts of the brain, they now have data that helps a great deal in understanding how lasting happiness can be created.

Dr Martin Seligman, Director of the University of Pennsylvania Positive Psychology Centre, has for the last 15 years been the driving force behind positive psychology and has popularized the idea that greater happiness is achievable and can be taught. The Positive Psychology Network funds more than 50 research groups involving more than 150 scientists from universities all over the world. It focuses on the empirical study of positive emotions, positive character traits and the institutions that can enable them to flourish such as democracy, the family etc. Positive Psychology courses are now offered at both American and European universities, and even schools now have it on the curriculum. Thousands of teachers have now been trained in the US to help children be more positive, encouraging them to focus on their strong points and learning to persevere in difficult situations.

Seligman has gone even further, believing we can all help ourselves to 'flourish' and have a better life. In his most recent book, *Flourish: A new understanding of happiness and wellbeing – and how to achieve them*, a manifesto for a science of well-being, he argues that measuring 'flourishing' produces a more meaningful guide to what is going on in a society than other markers. Whereas happiness has to do with positive emotion, engagement and fulfilment, he adds positive relationship and accomplishment into the mix for true well-being and 'flourishing'. He maintains that our characters can be developed through positive psychology – we can become wiser, stronger, more resilient and capable of dealing with rejection and failure; we can also become more self-disciplined and more generous to others.

In the UK Dr Anthony Seldon is well known for his innovative approach at the public school Wellington College where he has driven up academic standards and put well-being and positive thinking into the curriculum. Some state schools are also teaching well-being and happiness, training children in resilience, using techniques developed in behavioural therapy. This appears to help in raising IQs, giving pupils a happier outlook and more social skills and ensuring they are better able to handle adversity than other children. It is also more likely to produce responsible and thoughtful citizens ultimately. The UK Resilience Programme (building on the Pennsylvania Resiliency Programme developed and tested at the University of Pennsylvania) is conducting the largest trial of this approach in any country so far.

Many policy areas are being rethought since happiness brings many benefits, quite apart from feeling good - enhanced confidence, generally more successful and socially engaged citizens, people are healthier and tend to live longer. The Young Foundation, which works to tackle major social needs in the UK, produced The State of Happiness Report after 3 years of exploring how local government can practically improve the happiness and wellbeing of the nation. This has helped the idea of well-being to be incorporated into UK public policy.

Various independent initiatives are helping to change the climate. In April 2011 Action for Happiness ('a new mass movement to create a happier society') was launched as an independent non-profit organization. Lord Richard Layard is a leading economist and founder of the Centre for Economic Performance at the London School of Economics who believes that the happiness of society does not necessarily equate to income. (His book *Happiness: Lessons from a New Science* was published in 2005.) His co-founders are Geoff Mulgan, CEO of the Young Foundation and Dr Anthony Seldon. The aim of the organization is to help create a happier society, and to that end they are providing practical ideas to inspire people to take control of their own happiness and promoting a more optimistic view of what life could be like, as well as documenting real human experiences and examples for people to consider, for example, performing kind deeds for strangers, taking up exercise and learning simple meditation techniques. 'There's a positive, hopeful, quite empowering message,' says Mark Williamson, the director of Action for Happiness, 'from research, which shows that although our genes, upbringing and material circumstances are things that are outside our control in many ways, there's a really significant proportion of our happiness – perhaps as much as 40% - that comes from the way we choose to approach our lives.'

The LSE's Department of Geography and Environment and the Grantham Research Institute on Climate Change and the Environment have created a free iPhone app for happiness mapping - mappiness – to measure individual wellbeing across time and space. The app beeps users at random moments one or more times a day, asking how happy, relaxed and awake they feel using sliding scales. It also asks for contextual information on activity, companionship and location. Their hope is that they will find better answers to questions about the impact of geographic, climate and social interaction on happiness.

The Equality Trust, which has grown out of the work by the authors of *The Spirit Level*, is an independent campaign working to reduce income inequality and thus improve people's quality of life. It is working with others to build a social movement for change, disseminating the latest research, promoting evidence-based arguments and supporting a dynamic network of campaign groups across the UK.

Good work has long been done by The Prince's Trust, founded in 1976 by the Prince of Wales, and dedicated to improving the lives of disadvantaged young people in the UK. With youth unemployment increasing, and lost productivity and youth crime costing the economy a huge amount of money, the Trust runs programmes that encourage young people to take responsibility for themselves, and helps to develop key skills, confidence and motivation.

The Organization of Economic Co-operation and Development (OECD) has a global project on measuring the progress of societies, taking account of social, environmental and economic concerns rather than focusing mainly on economic indicators. The Better Life Index compares data for the 34 countries belonging to the OECD. In May 2011 Britain ranked 15th out of 34, with Denmark the happiest, followed by Canada, Norway and Sweden. Well-being is now an explicit goal of policy in various countries – rich and poor, at the local, regional and national levels

The New Economics Foundation (NEF) has proposed a new way of measuring social progress in modern societies – The National Accounts of Wellbeing. Based on the subjective wellbeing of citizens (their experiences, feelings and perceptions of how their lives are going), NEF suggests that such indicators will be far better than purely economic ones like Gross Domestic Product (GDP) as a measurement of how societies are faring. GDP was introduced in the 1930s, when the issue for many was survival. Nowadays most people have, by comparison with then, enough, but the whole issue of how people feel remains problematic. In the UK there has been a recognition that we need to shift from measuring growth and productivity alone to endeavouring to measure well-being if we want to measure a nation's success. The Office of National Statistics (ONS) is carrying out a survey for the British Government asking how people feel, how anxious, how satisfied with life, etc. How the happiness index will link to policy remains to be seen but it is at least a step in the right direction.

There is a growing international movement exploring what it might mean to capture the measures of well-being, not simply material wealth. Other projects endeavouring to develop better measures of well-being and progress include WellBeBe in Belgium, QUARS in Italy, the Canadian Index of Wellbeing, and the Bhutanese indicator of Gross National Happiness – GNH. This policy was established in the 1980s in the Himalayan kingdom of Bhutan by its king at the time, and unlike GDP (Gross Domestic Product), GNH measures the happiness of the people of Bhutan as an indicator of development and progress. While Bhutan might be seen as an under-developed country, there is no homelessness, no severe poverty – every family has land, livestock, a weaving loom and can meet most of its needs. There is also free health care and education for all. The government of Bhutan has made it its policy to balance industry and tourism, without destroying the environment and preserving the Bhutanese culture.

With a different vision we too can start to become a more altruistic society that is capable of transforming itself so that all will benefit. Each one of us must play our part. Everyone seeks to be happy but people have to agree to commit themselves to making general well-being a priority. Hopefully we have now reached a point where we can understand how necessary this is. The crisis of consciousness we are experiencing is forcing us to evolve and change our ways. As we wake up to the need for transformation we begin to understand that each one of us counts in these times of transition, and that changing our attitudes and behaviours and making different choices brings its own rewards as well as contributing to a better society and a better world for all. We can choose simpler lifestyles, we can choose to spend our money more ethically, to enjoy our leisure-time differently, in more satisfying ways that will more likely be better for our health and well-being and even our longevity. We can choose to be rooted in our communities and take more responsibility for decisions that have to be made, and play our part in helping others.

The people of Okinawa, an island archipelago in southern Japan, are a great example of getting it right. They are famous for being some of the longest-lived people in the world. They have the highest percentage of centenarians in the world and some of the lowest statistics for disease. Apart from their healthy diet, it's also true that they have a lifestyle which is key to their longevity and which emphasizes community and co-operation, caring and sharing. With the ageing demographic presenting society in the West with an immense challenge for the future, we would do well to understand this relationship between health, well-being and community

The new science of positive psychology shows that well-being can be lastingly increased. Compassion for others is an important aspect of wellbeing. Being kind to ourselves helps us to be kind to others, so it's a win-win way of life. Since 2001 The Greater Good Science Centre based at the University of California, Berkeley, has been at the forefront in terms of exploring the science of a happy and meaningful life and in disseminating its findings to the general public, first via its print magazine, Greater Good, and then via its website making available hundreds of articles, videos, podcasts, as well as forums to facilitate discussion and make connections within the online community.

The Charter for Compassion is another initiative to help change society, and be a force for good, regardless of religion. It is very much a co-operative effort and calls upon people everywhere to undertake creative, practical and sustained action to help solve the many problems which face us. Living with compassion is vital in our globalized world where everybody has become our neighbour. The Charter is inspiring compassionate action around the world.

Another rather different way in which people can feel happier and more connected is reflected in the Slow Movement. In the past people felt connected to their wider family and community and life was slower with more time for conversation. With less movement around a country for jobs, and a life that was lived more rurally than in cities, people felt more connected to place and to nature and its processes. Food was an important part of life in the past, with much of an income going to feeding the family, and many had a vegetable patch and kept animals. Food was often prepared together and not eaten on the hoof but around a table with shared conversations and debate. The Slow Movement is 'a worldwide movement to recapture this state of connectedness'. Our huge technological advances which save us time don't seem to have made us any less busy. In fact our lives have speeded up and been filled with yet more activity.

Many people feel uneasy about the fast pace of modern life. The Slow Movement began with Carlo Petrini's protest against the opening of a fast-food chain restaurant in Piazza di Spagna in Rome. This resulted in the founding of the Slow Food organization which seeks to encourage the enjoyment of regional produce, traditional foods, often grown organically. Other offshoot organizations include slow gardening, slow parenting, slow travel and even slow art and fashion.

In the UK the British coalition government via 'Cameron's Big Society' is an attempt to bring about change in society both by reducing the amount of state control and at the same time reviving civic life by members of the public enriching public services. While some of this is as much about more service for less money in an effort to reduce the national debt, there is a genuine desire to make radical change in the interest of creating a better society, with volunteers doing more in the health, education and social services arenas. The huge amount of public spending under the previous Labour government, and the expansion of the state since the 1960s, have had a negative effect on personal and social responsibility, making for a society which seems to have lost its way.

The 'Big Society is about transferring power from the centre to individuals, neighbourhoods, etc. – whatever is appropriate. There will be a new focus on 'empowering and enabling individuals, families and communities to take control of their lives so we create the avenues through which responsibility and opportunity can develop'. (Cameron). There are plenty of examples of community regeneration where local councils have managed to engage residents and neighbourhoods in taking an active role in improving their areas, for example Balsall Heath and Castle Vale in Birmingham, which has demonstrated over the last 20 years how the idealism of the 'Big Society' might translate into reality with residents coming together and improving their lives and surroundings (Civic Streets Report).

Volunteering is an increasingly important aspect of community enriching public services. Dame Elisabeth Hoodless, the executive director of Community Service Volunteers (CSV), the volunteering charity, has spoken of how trained and screened volunteers of all ages are already helping to reduce crime and improve health and social care. In Bromley, Lewisham, Southend, Islington and Coventry volunteers attached to families with children on the 'at risk' register are achieving remarkable results, saving money as well as helping to improve the quality of people's lives. Youth crime is being tackled too through mentors supporting young people who are at risk of becoming offenders or are already in trouble, and many have been successfully diverted from crime. CSV also organizes neighbourhood volunteers to help support frail elderly people who prefer to stay in their own homes. Likewise volunteers can help raise the level of care available in hospitals, or provide personalized and supportive transport to appointments at hospitals or GPs' surgeries. Other volunteers organize healthy walks or health education programmes or make regular visits to isolated patients. Research has demonstrated that huge savings have been made as a result of volunteer efforts, and it seems plausible that much more money could be saved if such initiatives were rolled out across the country.

In August 2011 the world was shocked to see riots in London and other cities in England, and subsequent to this there has been much discussion about how to prevent such violence. Both volunteering and mentoring have been shown to really make a difference to young people who feel alienated and hopeless. While improving social conditions is important, getting young people involved in voluntary work in their communities can help them become more responsible and disciplined. In *Redirect: the surprising new science of psychological change*, Timothy Wilson, Professor of Psychology at the University of Virginia, shows how it is possible to deal with social problems through changing one's way of looking at life and redirecting thought processes to become more optimistic. Disenfranchised kids can be taught to view their lives differently.

One initiative in the UK that offers hope is the new National Citizen Service. About 9000 16-year-olds took part in pilot schemes in the summer of 2011, and the plan is for a further 30,000 to be involved in 2012. The citizen service is a 3-week scheme, which includes 2 weeks away from home, first on an outdoor activity course and then volunteering in a neighbourhood, and a third week designing a social action project. People from different social classes and backgrounds work together, and the hope is that the scheme increases self-esteem and self-confidence and makes more productive and better socially oriented citizens. In the long term such people are less likely to commit crime and are more likely to be employable.

More of such schemes and initiatives are needed, but for this to happen the British government recognizes that social entrepreneurs and community activists, as well as the population at large, have to be enthusiastic and prepared to be actively involved. The internet will be important in stimulating this. To that end the government has set up a website, Your Square Mile, to enable all the citizens in the UK to make changes in as many of the 93,000 square miles in the country as possible, by getting involved in local projects, reporting problems that need dealing with in the community etc.. There are approximately 900,000 community groups in the UK and 238,000 social entrepreneurs. The government wants to link these groups and communities via this initiative to enable the sharing of ideas and resources so that all citizens will be able to benefit.

II

Three themes run through this chapter – consciousness, community and connection. Social networks were integral to developing societies from earliest times, whether through strong links from close relationships with family and friends, or looser links to the wider community. They had an important effect on our development as a species, enabling us to co-operate in large groups and create extraordinary large-scale societies. Now we have online social networks as well as real social networks, and these online networks of both immediate and peripheral links can be tremendously powerful, particularly with the opportunities and challenges we face today. The Internet, together with mobile phones and social networking sites like Facebook, Twitter and YouTube have become the 'connective tissue' of our society, writes Clay Shirky, the leading expert on social and technological networks, in *Cognitive Surplus*. Interconnection is a natural and necessary part of our lives, and we have the ability as never before to stay in touch, share information, interact and achieve our goals through vast networks of links. We have become 'hyperconnected'. Blogging, microblogging (Twitter) and Vlogging (video blogging) means communication is no longer passive – anyone can put their ideas out there for others to respond to. Social TV networking means producers are switching to social networking with apps that allow viewers to comment and influence what they are watching. Academics now get help with their research, using smart-phone technology to take crowd-sourcing (outsourcing tasks to the public) to a new level of interactivity, with apps to help record for example events in the natural world that are being monitored.

We now have the ability to make a new world. The

Internet and social media networks are becoming hugely instrumental in changing culture, enabling us to create new kinds of communities effortlessly. Social networks have the power to do things which no single person can do on their own. They can be a tremendous force for good because they are part of what has become a giant superorganism, where millions of people have integrated the use of social networking sites into their daily lives. As well as making information universally available, everyone has been given a voice. Even those who don't have access themselves can benefit. For example, in India in the fight against corruption, bribery has been made transparent by the website ipaidabribe.com. The impact has been felt by those who are not using the site because corruption is at last being challenged and people are beginning to understand their rights, so that they and others are not forced to pay bribes.

Networked individuals, once they become a critical mass, have the power to hold government responsible. Social networks can have profound effects too on the way we govern ourselves. They can be used to win elections, as Obama did with the social networking site, National Field, in the US in 2008, which kept the campaign up-to-date with election data and voter feedback. They can also be used to organize demonstrations, as in the Arab Spring in

2011 when activists posted on Facebook and Twitter to inform others as to what was happening, and downloading scenes captured on their mobiles to YouTube. These were then broadcast around the world and a global network of supporters was built up as the world watched the progress of the revolutions and the overthrow of corrupt regimes. Social networks therefore can spread information to millions rapidly and have power to be emancipatory, spreading individual freedom. They have become an agency for global change with closed societies being opened up and citizens being empowered to speak freely and co-ordinate politically.

Eric Schmidt, CEO of Google, maintains that 'the internet is the greatest force for good in the world', and certainly the new online networks can help change the culture by spreading healthy behaviour and positive attitudes, addressing personal growth and environmental issues, working for human rights and world-wide peace etc. Individuals can also be 'nudged' to make a decision that will be beneficial for them. There's no need for coercion or bans, it's just a question of being given the facts and the options.

However, some feel that there has been too much euphoria about the potential of the internet and social media, and certainly we shouldn't ignore the dangers. The issue of 'cyberutopians' v. the 'cybercons' has been addressed by Evgeny Morozov in The *Net Delusion: The Dark Side of Internet Freedom*. Although there is great benefit, with citizens becoming empowered and hope and inspiration spread, so too can anxiety and panic be contagious, for example, in the financial markets. Worse still, cyber crime has become a new type of serious globally organized crime, whether credit and bank card hacking - through websites such as Dark Market (now closed down); or information being illegally procured and sold (industrial espionage); or all-out cyber warfare where computer systems can be infiltrated and closed down. There is also the danger that the internet and social media can become agents of social control, with propaganda by authoritarian regimes, spying and rounding up of dissidents in countries like China and Iran. There is also concern about increased surveillance generally. Whatever we click on is stored in Silicon Valley so that we can be watched over more closely. Mark Zuckerberg, founder of Facebook, declared that ' privacy is dead', and indeed we're already monitored by CCTV, and now even tracked by cameras using 'smart eyes' in advertising hoardings to assess our potential as customers, which brings up the whole issue of corporate power and the use of private information for profit.

Some are also concerned about our dependence on networked systems and cyber overload. Nicholas Carr, the culture critic, has argued in *The Shallows: What the Internet is doing to our brain* that excessive use of the internet reshapes our brain structure because the brain retains a certain amount of plasticity throughout life. Elias Aboujaoude, a psychiatrist at Stanford University's School of Medicine, has written about his belief that we are being transformed psychologically and neurologically in his book *VirtuallyYou: The Dangerous Powers of the E-Personality*. He fears that in spite of many positive effects of the internet, many of us may be developing 'e-personalities', alternative personae which could become a factor in mental illness. Others feel that the decrease in face-to-face communication results in people being cocooned in virtual worlds, forming faux friendships and being unable to truly connect with others. There is also the issue of anonymous blogging, covert bullying or 'trolling' (troll is Old Norse for monster), all of which can cause immense harm. Finally, our ability to make decisions is becoming impacted by the vast amount of data we now handle in our wired lives – 'the internet is creating cognitive overload', according to Angela Dimoka, Director of the Centre for Neural Decision-Making at Temple University in Philadelphia.

It might seem as if our powers of concentration and

contemplation are diminishing and our stress levels are rising as we have less time for family and friends, but many people realize this and appreciate how necessary it is to find time to stop and think. We can't live in a permanent state of stimulation and distraction – sooner or later it catches up with us and we begin to feel less fulfilled, so digitally downsizing by cutting time online is an obvious solution. Reflection and creativity are in the end more beneficial than vast amounts of information. And the way we think can be reshaped for the better, just as much as for worse, as I have pointed out in chapter 3.

Overall it is a better world we live in because of the Internet. Negative effects are in a sense side effects that we have to deal with in order to get the gains. The downsides can be overcome. The culture can be changed, and is changing, and goodness and happiness can be spread. Jane McGonigal is a leading prophet of web positivity who teaches game design at the University of California, Berkeley, and she believes that online communities generally treat others as they want to be treated. She feels that we are 'moving towards a new form of collective intelligence'. The individual self is becoming less important as boundaries become blurred, and the good of the whole becomes more important. With a more relational consciousness developing, we might well see a new sense of empathy for others developing as evolution unfolds.

CHAPTER 5
Enlightened economics - creating socially responsible & enviromentally sustainable business

The collapse of Lehman Brothers in September 2008 and the ensuing financial crash plunged the world into an uncertain future. Boom had turned out not to have been boom, but rather reckless lending and borrowing without the ability to repay, whilst hedge fund speculators made fortunes from increasingly complex derivatives. Although attempts have been made to reform economic institutions and reduce the amount of debt in the industrialized world, the 'fault lines' in the global economic system remained, and the financial crisis has worsened. Global debt (including government, corporate and personal borrowing has mushroomed into hundreds of trillions of dollars as finance ministers endeavour to get a grip on the spiralling crisis. As I write the Eurozone crisis is still ongoing and it is not clear whether the Euro will survive. So intertwined is the global financial system that all will feel the effects whether in Europe, the US, or those economies which have until now been growing fast in countries like India and China. The debt of the US and the Eurozone is exacerbated too by problems which are becoming more obvious, like the ageing population which increases pensions and other liabilities, and the lack of employment for the young. The spectre of the 1930s with economic chaos, depression and civil unrest is beginning to haunt us. The loss of consumer, business and market confidence has resulted in a crisis of credibility, with indecision and politics compounding the problems. It has become an existential crisis as well as an economic one.

However, instead of fearing for the future, perhaps the crisis is the trumpet blast needed to force us to confront reality. Both the current economic system and we ourselves have to change. We need to rethink our attitudes towards both economic growth and consumption, and have to put people and the environment before profit. Many people are realizing this and around the world the protest movement is growing with Occupy spreading from Oakland and Wall Street to the City of London and way beyond, demanding a responsible or moral capitalism to address the inequalities in the system. Even in Russia and China the working people are challenging a system seen as unfair and corrupt.

We seem to have forgotten that economics is supposed to serve human ends and that banks are supposed to serve their communities, not just themselves. But it's not just the fault of the bankers – the whole culture needs to change. Yes, we need to build more resilient economies, but we also have to become more resilient as individuals, changing our values and expectations so that we're no longer burdened with debt, over-consuming, and destroying the environment.

For the last fifty to sixty years perpetual economic growth, with ever-increasing consumption of goods and resources, has been regarded as the holy grail in economics. This obsession with growth, and particularly with profit from that growth, is a fundamental flaw in our economic system. It is a myth and we have become collectively blind to its inherent dangers. Economic growth has been dependent on oil, gas and coal, but to keep burning them is to court disaster. Perpetual economic growth and ever greater profits are just not viable - certainly not to the extent that there are enough resources for everyone to live the kind of privileged lifestyle that those of us who live in industrialized societies do. Constantly having to chase profit has resulted in excessive competition between corporations and exploitation of both people and resources, particularly in the third world. The gap between rich and poor has escalated to a level which is simply unacceptable, whilst the resources of the earth have been plundered to the point where the ecological balance is dangerously out of kilter. Endlessly cutting costs in pursuit of profit has resulted in growing unemployment, whilst ever more consumption of things we are persuaded that we ' need', funded by borrowing and debt, has resulted in the dysfunctional society we have in the Western world.

In addition our civilization is facing unprecedented challenges such as the rising cost of extracting oil, increasing consumption of vital resources like water, climate change and a demographic time bomb of a world population estimated to rise from 7 billion to 9 billion by 2050. We have reached a point where we are being forced to think about the common good. As the Thai Buddhist, Sulak Sivaraksa, twice nominated for the Nobel Peace Prize and winner of the Right Livelihood Award, has written: 'Societies would be healthier if they advanced sustainability rather than unlimited growth, if they were places where people would help one another in hard times, where power would be shared rather than fought over, where nature would be revered rather than exploited, where spirituality and wisdom would be honoured.'

Capitalism has of course produced many benefits and is capable of producing benefit for all when wisely practised. Growth in itself is not necessarily bad. However, there is an underlying problem with our economic system which isn't immediately obvious but is vital to understand if we want to explore what a new, more enlightened, or conscious, economics might mean. This underlying problem is a perceptual one. It has to do with what we see as wealth. The word 'wealth' comes from the Old English word 'weal', meaning wellbeing. We tend to equate wealth with money, and see money as the key to satisfying all our needs and desires. But money cannot do this, for it is merely a form of exchange. We do not increase our self-worth because we have the wherewithal to buy whatever we want, and when we mistakenly think our wants are our needs. The word money actually derives from the Latin *moneta* meaning mint, the original epithet of the goddess Juno, patron goddess of Rome and the Roman empire, in whose temple in Rome the mint was housed. This sacred connection perhaps reminds us that money is meant to be used wisely both on our own account and for the common good. Since the traditional roles of the family, the church (or synagogue, mosque or temple) and the community as the supporters and upholders of moral values have broken down, our culture has become more selfish and self-indulgent.

The problem is that the Newtonian-Darwinian worldview that has become embedded in our consciousness and dominated our culture for so long is one in which only

the fittest survive - the winner takes all mentality.
Competition, materialistic values and assumptions drive us
just as much as the next man or woman, and just as much
as the financial institutions and global corporations we
tend to denounce as greedy and corrupt. But appreciation
of what we have, rather than constantly seeking more
money and goods, and then sharing with others, is what
matters. This enables people and communities to flourish.
It means we don't take more than we really need from the
environment whose diversity is our primary source of real
wealth and our most precious commodity. We need an
economic system that puts people, communities and the
environment first, not profit and endless GDP growth.

The word economics comes from the Greek word
oikonomos meaning household manager. In Ancient Greece it
was to do with the survival and wellbeing of every member
of the household, so from the very beginnings of Western
civilization economics was associated with ethics and
linked with faith, symbolism and trust. If we extrapolate
this out - from household, to village, to city and state, and
think of the entire planet as comparable to a household
- then the worldwide economy needs to work for all its
inhabitants. It's a moral issue. Not only must distribution
of wealth and opportunity meet the needs of everyone, it
must also be sustainable, meeting the needs of all forms of

life and of future generations. We have the resources and capability to feed, clothe and house the world's population – we just need to have the will to make this our priority.

An 'enlightened' economics means that a number of major issues need to be addressed:

1 /   Long-term reform of our financial system is required to create stability. David Korten, in *Agenda for A New Economy*, has described our current one as 'a money game in which players use money to make money for people who have money without producing anything of value'. Yet if wealth is about the common good, then those who control money have to be socially responsible and use money for the good of society and the environment. Only a small proportion of the world's population owns most of its money, and clearly we need a more equitable system of distribution. We need more ethical investment – socially responsible investment (SRI) which respects people, communities and the environment.

2 /   Restructuring of the rules governing corporations is necessary.   Globalization has meant more business opportunities but at enormous cost to people and the environment. There has to be corporate commitment to ethical principles, not just to the pursuit of profit and maximizing shareholder wealth. More has to be put back

into communities whilst at the same time protecting the environment. Alternatives should be considered too like employee stakes in a company and co-operatives.

3 /   Global imbalances need to be reduced. In 1950 the rich world per capita income was 20 times that of the poorest fifth of the world's population. Now it is 80 times. The gap between rich and poor has to be addressed. We don't need to have poverty on the scale which we do. There are enough resources, even in Africa, where the problem is more to do with corrupt governments. Even in the West the gap between rich and poor has grown in spite of increased rises in GDP because those who already have the wealth have taken most of the gains, as seen in the extraordinary increase in earnings differential between the lowest and highest paid in business and institutions. For example, in the UK (September 2011) the High Pay Commission reported that the total pay packages for executives in FTS 350 companies had gone up 700% since 2002 while pay levels for the average worker had increased by only 27%.

4 /   Unsustainability issues have to be resolved. We cannot continue to exploit the environment for our own ends, plundering the earth's resources and damaging nature's eco-system with our waste. We have to have

low-carbon sustainable business practices that protect the environment, with the developed world taking the largest share of the cost, and we need to change our own patterns of consuming and waste disposal.

5 /	Regulation - government policies need to address this. Some see the free enterprise market as the problem and argue for more regulation and restrictions on individual freedom; and zero growth. Others argue for keeping the markets open and being free to do what we like: with yet more growth. Some see localization as the answer with local small farms and community supported agriculture and business. Others argue that the big emerging economies of the BRICS (Brazil, Russia, India and China) and the new group of countries called the CIVETS (Colombia, Indonesia, Venezuela, Egypt, Turkey and south Africa) present a huge opportunity, and with greater mobility and adaptability within the free market there can be more creativity and technological innovation, ultimately leading to more enterprise and trade and new patterns of living. There are no easy answers, but the issue of regulation has to be dealt with.

6 /	Individual responsibility – we need to rethink our consumer lifestyle and the way income is distributed. We all need to choose simpler lifestyles. As Gandhi

put it so memorably – 'Live simply that others may simply live.' Whilst supporting the unemployed and disadvantaged to cover basic needs, this has to be linked with incentives for responsible and creative lifestyles, for example, volunteering. At the same time we need equal opportunities for all to use their talents, improving educational access for everyone so that we have the appropriate skills for the modern workplace.

7 /   We need different economic indicators. Increased GDP (Gross Domestic Product) does not increase quality of life, as we have seen (see chapter 4). Economists assess economic performance by growth in GDP, a measure of the market value of economic output, but this does not measure other forms of contribution, whether it is women's work in the home, caring for children or relatives, or the 'free' resources of the planet like sea and lakes. Various alternatives which replace GDP with non-financial indicators of social and environmental health have been suggested, such as GNH (Gross National Happiness) or the National Account of Wellbeing.

So if these are the main issues, what are the signs that we are moving towards a more conscious economic system? Can we take hope from what we see happening around the world? In spite of the turmoil there does seem to be a shift taking place, with very real efforts to build a different kind of economic future based on ethical, sustainable principles rather than on risky financial bets and fierce competition.

Socially responsible investing (SRI) is growing with professionally managed assets following SRI strategies increasing dramatically. SRI funds tend to avoid companies that produce firearms, nuclear power, tobacco or alcohol, or do not employ fair labour practices, discriminate against women, minorities etc. Shareholders are pressurizing major corporations to be more socially responsible through shareholder resolutions and divestment campaigns. Community investing encourages people to invest in valuable land projects such as rehabilitating abandoned buildings in run-down areas. Socially responsible venture capital investors are also investing in start-up companies that use business to solve social problems.

Corporations and businesses are being forced to change, whether because of the toughness of the economic situation, growing pressure to adopt sustainable policies, the retention of talented people, or demands from consumers on quality and price. A new breed of CEOs, employees and consumers is emerging. Businesses are no longer solely focused on generating profit and pushing for growth at the expense of people and the environment. Instead of the single bottom line, it's the triple bottom line – people, planet, profit – creating more transparency and accountability in the process.

In building a new integrity and trust after all the corporate corruption scandals companies are very keen to be seen as socially responsible, which means giving back to the community and supporting community projects. They also want to be seen as environmentally sustainable which means having policies which protect rather than manipulate the environment. In many businesses now there is a different style of leadership, more aware CEOs who understand that individuals within corporations have to be empowered and inspired to grow and express their creativity. Employees want a greater sense of meaning and purpose in their work life, and when encouraged to express their creativity and fulfil their potential, they are more likely to come up with innovative ideas. They are also more inclined to stay in their jobs and work harder and smarter. There are now many in the middle ranks of corporations who are highly motivated and believe they can make a contribution in both work and the community.

Opportunities for personal development and community service have made a real difference. Change initiatives have been rolled out way beyond business too into other kinds of organizations like government departments, schools and universities, hospitals etc. – all helping to tap into people's full capacity and make more responsible citizens contributing to society. People and organizations are transforming themselves and waking up to a different way of behaving. Concern for employee welfare, as well as concern for the bottom line, has resulted in stress management techniques, or transformational tools like Neurolinguistic Programming (NLP) and visualization being introduced in many companies, for example, Apple, Google, Yahoo and AOL all sponsor meditation in the workplace.

In some areas the whole concept of work is changing too as people work at different activities, work shorter working weeks or have blocks of time in work and then in recreational activities which might well include volunteering. The New Economic Foundation's 21 Hours Report argues that with less growth in the economy of the future there are less tax revenues to invest in health, education, social care and other essential services. We have to change our entrenched ideas about the value of paid and unpaid work and need to work towards distributing both more equally across the adult population, releasing resources to help each other more. For argument's sake, 21 hours has been proposed as the ideal for paid work – not necessarily 3 7-hour days, but perhaps the equivalent of 1092 hours across a calendar year with a range of options as to how hours are worked. According to the report, many of the crises we face would be solved – unemployment would decrease, over-consumption would reduce, high carbon emissions would go down, inequality would become less, overwork and stress would be a thing of the past, and general wellbeing would improve with us all having more time to enjoy life and make a greater contribution to society, as well as living more sustainably.

One thing certainly seems to be happening, and that is that our working consciousness is changing dramatically. The future of how we all work may be difficult to predict, but we can be sure that technological changes will continue to transform the world of work, that globalization will continue to have a major effect on us, as will changing demographics and longer life-spans. There are likely to be plenty of opportunities and more choice, with knowledge, creativity and innovation being the basis by which many people choose to make their living in the future. Many more people are likely to work for themselves, or with smaller groups of people, but they will also be connected to the know-how, competencies and networks of others.

While some have already adapted to new patterns of

working, others are completely changing their careers. Some City high-fliers are no longer interested in the top jobs with large salaries, but instead are choosing job satisfaction, a happy family life and emotional well-being. They are taking on roles within smaller organizations or becoming entrepreneurs. Some are becoming farmers, others retraining as teachers. There is a shift away from a way of working that is all-consuming to a more balanced and meaningful employment.

There is also a whole new breed of young environmental crusaders and entrepreneurs, for example, the wealthy David de Rothschild on his yacht Plastiki, a 60-foot catamaran made entirely of recycled plastic bottles, crossed the Pacific to put pollution under the spotlight. Blake Mycoskie, founder of TOMS Shoes, built his business after seeing bare-foot children in Argentina, and now TOMS donates a new pair of shoes to a child in need of shoes for every pair of shoes it sells. NIKA Water Company uses 100% of its profits from the sales of bottled water in the USA to provide clean water to those in the developing world. Social entrepreneurs are becoming more important and programmes on how to become a social entrepreneur are being run at some of the leading business schools.

We seem to be in the midst of a real values revolution, a

profound shift in how we spend our time and money, with consumers expecting greater accountability. The culture of acquisition where we spent more than we earned prior to 2008 has given way to a more thoughtful consumption. People prefer pay-as-you-go living, using debit rather than credit cards. They want brands with integrity, social responsibility and sustainability at their heart. The positive side of the various crises we face is that consumers are making different choices about what they purchase. There is a realization that how we choose to spend money is a form of power, and consumers are using it to communicate their values and spend with those companies who share their values. More thoughtful spending forces businesses to deliver higher quality and more responsible behaviour. Millions of individuals want a better and fairer world for all and they don't want products that pollute the planet. They want purchases which do not exploit the poor and take away their chance of growing their own crops, and they want goods which are ecologically sound. The Fair Trade movement is growing in strength and sweat shops are shunned. There is a recognition that we are all connected and that we become more fully human by working together and helping one another. The future is about co-operation, not competition. Organic food, eco-fashion and eco-tourism are growing steadily as are alternative health and cosmetic care products and cleaning products – all of which are better for health as well as for the planet. Another economic manifestation of the reaction to mass consumption is 'collaborative consumption', based on sharing, collaboration and community. Bartering, exchanging, renting, lending or other such ways of more efficiently using what they have, enables individuals to consume efficiently, save money and help the environment, as well as becoming more connected with each other in the process. At the grass-roots level people are well ahead of politicians, institutions and corporations. This is not just an internet phenomenon, though the internet is hugely important in enabling people to make better choices, but it also involves networks of all kinds. Consumers are taking more into their own hands and getting much longed for meaning and connection into their lives as well as fulfilling their needs for products and services. There are, for example, Time banks where people can trade their time, eg. a chef can prepare a meal for a plumber, who reciprocates by fixing the shower. In Japan one system that has become very popular with the growing elderly population is *fureai kippu*, meaning caring relationship ticket. In return for helping the elderly who do not have health insurance with everyday tasks, you can earn credits which go into a fureai kippu savings account. You can either draw on this when you yourself are old or you can transfer the credits to an elderly relative for them to use.

Sometimes there are just very informal arrangements within communities, eg. my local florist supplies flowers and plants to local shops and cafes in return for a haircut or beauty treatment or lunch. A farmer might supply a haunch of venison in return for some fencing. This kind of exchange is happening much more than we perhaps realize – no money changes hands, tax is avoided and unneccesary car trips to shops or supermarkets are avoided. Heyneighbor.co, big in the US, is redefining what a neighbour is – you can start an online community, where you can post a request for help with something like setting up broadband or asking for recipes to deal with a glut of apples.

Much of this kind of exchange is happening through the internet and smart phones. Thousands of people are now choosing to hire household items through websites such as Ecomodo, Rentmyitems and Zilok – a cheaper or greener way of sourcing DIY equipment or garden machinery. There is a definite trend towards people wanting to pay for the use of an item rather than owning it. Zipcar is a car-sharing service, and Hourbike operates a number of key bike-sharing schemes in the UK with its pay-as-you-go cycle network (bike-sharing is now the fastest growing form of transport in the world). ParkatmyHouse.

com allows people to make money from unused space outside their properties. Couchsurfing.com offers 'couch' accommodation for visitors and travellers. Airbnb is also a popular site for accommodation, as are Crashpadder and Room-arama. You don't even have to do a direct swap – you can stay with one member and let your home to another.

Other popular websites are those offering discounted products and services, like Groupon, the biggest and best known, which started in Chicago in 2008 and has now spread to 43 countries. The idea is that businesses are invited to offer discounts, and individuals to take up the offers. A daily deal is offered for each city in which it operates. The discounts happen once a certain number of people agree to pay for the coupon or 'groupon' that gives them the special price. This could be a meal out worth £50 for £20, or £150 spa experience for £50. For consumers this means low prices and for business the theory is it creates and expands the market at low cost. True, there have been complaints about discount websites delivering, and some businesses see it as a costly promotion since hardly any Groupon customers come back, but in these challenging times experimentation is key and worth the risk.

Even big consumer brands like Nike are shifting their brand focus and advertising towards building collaborative communities investing in non-media social hubs like NikePlus, where runners around the world post running routes, map their runs and offer advice.

Along with more mindful consumption, consumers are choosing simpler lifestyles that include thrift, downshifting and even voluntary simplicity. The reality is people are increasingly happy not just to work less but also to use their leisure more creatively. Simpler and greener approaches to living are becoming part of everyday life and culture, from organic gardening and farming to healthier home cooking, to sewing and knitting.   People are happy to help friends and neighbours, undertake volunteer work, work on allotments to grow their own organic food, keep chickens and bees etc. Community farms and gardens are a growing phenomenon, mainly in urban areas and projects range from tiny wildlife gardens to vegetable plots on housing estates, polytunnels and larger city farms. There is an increasing emphasis on rebuilding communities with people working together to improve shared living and working space, for example, Detroit, symbol of the decline of industrial culture, has become a beacon of hope as grassroots efforts to build community gardens are beginning to transform the city. In Berlin there are 80,000 community gardens. The numbers are growing in the UK too. In London there are now many community garden projects such as the one in the borough of Islington, King Henry Walk Gardens, supported by Islington Council, which has been created by local volunteers for the local community. Capital Growth is a scheme instigated by London's Mayor, Boris Johnson with Rosie Boycott, the Chair of the London Food Board. The aim is to have over 2000 spaces from corners of school playgrounds, parks and council estates adapted for vegetable growing. There are many examples of such initiatives which are making a real difference to people's lives, enabling stronger community relationships, building self-esteem and giving social support, in addition to fresh food and exercise. The same spirit of wanting to have a greener lifestyle means that people are driving less and sharing cars when they can, they are using public transport more, bicycling and walking more.

Above all there is a realization by many in the western world that our affluent lifestyle has not brought health and happiness and that there are more satisfying ways of living. Connecting, sharing and putting energy into building community seems so much better than competing and consuming. One of the initiatives to adapting and thriving is the Transition Movement which has revitalized many local communities. There are now 320 communities -

villages, small towns, council districts, cities and boroughs – in the UK, USA, Canada, Australia, New Zealand, Italy and Chile... The idea of a Transition culture grew out of the work of permaculture designer, Rob Hopkins in Kinsale, Ireland, where he successfully created an Energy Descent Plan which was adopted by the town council as policy. The first Transition Towns plan was launched in Totnes in Devon in conjunction with the local authority in 2006. The movement has a strikingly practical and optimistic approach to sustainability. The overall aim is to raise awareness of sustainable living to build local resilience. To counter the rising cost of oil prices and climate change, as well as helping deal with the general rise in food prices, the movement's objectives for local communities are:

1 /   to grow more food locally
2 /   to generate a community's own power
3 /   to build houses using local materials
4 /   to reduce waste
5 /   to encourage the development of local currencies, and keep money in the local area.

Local self-sufficiency is also an important factor in the Buy-local and Grow-local movements. There are clearly huge advantages to buying locally produced goods:

1 /   the elimination or reduction of transportation costs

2 /   support of the local economy, recirculating money
       so that it is spent locally instead of being spent
       outside the community

3 /   the improvement of the quality of life in the locality
       because money has been retained for the
       community

4 /   additional benefits in the case of food production
of provenance, less deterioration, and eating seasonally.
Food can of course be grown successfully anywhere,
even in the bleakest of city environments, as many of the
community garden initiatives from Detroit to Berlin to
London demonstrate.

Of all the various initiatives revitalizing communities
Local Exchange Trading Systems (LETS) is well established
with over 1500 groups worldwide in 39 countries. It
is a community information system where people and
groups of people (charities, voluntary groups, housing
co-operatives etc.) agree to exchange goods and services
with each other without the need for cash. LETS networks
use interest-free local credit. As credit is issued by the
network members, for the benefit of the members, LETS
are considered mutual credit systems. There is great
variation between schemes and although they can help
revitalize and build community they are not without their
challenges.

As we move through the period of change and adaptation, initiatives are not without their problems. As long as human beings are involved, there will always be challenges! One example of this is in the field of microfinance. Microfinance, or microcredit, aims to help poor people start their own business or make other worthwhile investments like getting an education. It tends to be given to groups rather than individuals and is largely employed in the third world, though programmes have been put into practice even in the industrialized West. The best-known microfinance institution is the Grameen bank in Bangladesh, founded 35 years ago by the economist and Nobel peace-prize winner, Muhammad Yunus, who pioneered microcredit, making tiny loans to some of the poorest people in Bangladesh. Since then 128 million people have received a microloan and largely been helped to get themselves out of poverty. However, there is now a great deal of controversy surrounding the Grameen Bank and its activities following a series of suicides by rural borrowers in Andhra Pradesh in India as a result of some over-zealous debt-collectors. Some are even questioning whether microfinance does break the cycle of poverty. It would seem that microfinance as a concept is sound but that what really is at issue is a more ethical system of lending and collecting, plus whether the people receiving the loan have the skills to utilize it. It might also be that the poor need to have access to a range of financial services not just microcredit, but including insurance, savings and micro-franchising etc. Certainly microfinance is preferable to Aid or charity since in the long-term it helps people to thrive rather than just survive. Microfinance, like anything else, will have its risks and limitations, but overall its effects have been beneficial and a means for self-empowerment.

So whether we look at different ways of banking or running business, at communities endeavouring to work together in new creative ways, or at consumers earning their livelihood and spending their money more consciously, clearly the signs of change for a better world are all around us. The social scientist/urban studies theorist, Richard Florida, has termed this 'the Great Reset'. "What economic crises do is reset the conditions for technological innovation and consumption and demand." Arguing that all organisms and systems go through cycles of life, death and rebirth, he sees both the depressions of the 1870s and the 1930s as giving rise to enormous creativity and vastly improved living standards. In *The Great Reset: How new ways of living and working drive post-crash prosperity*, he demonstrates how creativity and innovation are our greatest hope for the future, leading to new patterns of living, working and consuming.

We can solve the economic crises we face by working together, but we have to let go of what no longer works and reframe the challenges. Put a different way, we have to change the lens through which we view the world. We have a choice about how we see the world around us and we have a choice about the culture we create going forward. With a new consciousness of wisdom and compassion we can choose behaviour that is honest, caring, sharing and co-operative rather than behaviour which makes us competitive, selfish and greedy. We can rebuild our economies, our communities and change our culture and institutions over time, and with this intention, and the means through the internet, smart phones and social media, a more enlightened economics which is already in the process of developing, can become a reality.

CHAPTER 6
A new kind of politics - seeking the highest common good

When a culture is undergoing some kind of transformation, politics tends to be the last bastion of the old order to react, following changes in society and in the economic arena. Wherever you look in the world today governments and politicians are not seen as trustworthy. Rather they are viewed as preoccupied with manipulating public opinion, winning elections and hanging on to power, some sadly by whatever unethical or evil means it takes.

Electorates are disillusioned (reflected in low turnouts when voting, especially in the West), whether because of corruption, lies, manipulation, incompetence or simply failure to listen to what people need. Often, even if they are politically engaged, voters are not inspired by their leaders with their empty rhetoric and short-term approaches to important issues. The dominance of masculine values and the lack of real wisdom amongst politicians preclude a more meaningful politics which many voters long for.

Worse still, where dictators have been entrenched for

years, as in those countries of Africa which hold supposedly democratic elections, for example Zimbabwe or Kenya, the electorate fear them; or in countries where there exists ruthless authoritarianism, as in China, the people put up with it for fear of unleashing chaos. History has shown the price to be paid for freedom, while the Arab Spring in North Africa and the Middle East provides a more recent example of how in the end there is always revolution against corrupt governments and rulers, with people prepared to die to secure a better future for their children.

Even in the Western world we now have growing signs of unrest. The Occupy Movement protested in hundreds of our cities. Beginning on 17 September 2011 in Zucotti Park, New York, as a protest against social and economic inequality, against greed and corruption, particularly on Wall Street, Occupy has helped in the growing awareness of the cracks in our social and political systems. Capitalism and democracy have been found wanting, but as people begin to demand change and the issues are more hotly debated, then it is more likely that governments will have to change and we can have a revitalized democracy.

Whether Western liberal democracy will become the ultimate form of human government, as political scientist Francis Fukuyama has postulated, remains to be seen. In spite of the problems confronting it, democracy is still the best form of government that has ever existed, though it has taken many different forms since its earliest days. That is the strength of, and the hope for, democracy since it is able to adapt and change. While others around the world aspire to more democratic regimes, how come we in the West, blessed with liberal democracy, have arrived at such a point of disenchantment? Over the last 30 years the international global network of finance has become the power-house and increasingly national governments have centralized power within their own countries. This has left people feeling that there is little opportunity for citizen participation.

There is however a deeper reason as to why this disenchantment has arisen, and that is to do with how we view the world. For most of history the human race has tended to see itself as an integral part of the natural world, but for the last 400 years the Newtonian-Darwinian worldview has come to be the dominant one. This rational, scientific, reductionist approach to everything means that order and control take precedence over meaning. We no longer see the world in cosmic terms, where time is circular and seasonal, but we want to see objectively, and this creates separation and disconnection. Instead of seeing ourselves as part of a whole, we've all become separate individuals in a world where only the fittest survive.

Discoveries in the new physics however have shown us that viewing the world from a Newtonian-Darwinian perspective is outmoded. We now know that every quantum is connected to every other quantum, and every organism with the organisms in the eco-system. Nothing exists in isolation, we are not separate but part of the whole, and everything we do has an effect elsewhere. Our relationship to the cosmos is becoming better understood as we see the damage the old worldview has caused.

Social and political philosophers like Steve McIntosh and Ken Wilber believe we are in the midst of a huge 'paradigm shift', where the old worldview is giving way to the new. This emerging worldview has been described by them as 'integral', in other words it's more holistic, one of a more aware consciousness, which has 'more energy for life, more compassion for others, more personal power and strategic wisdom'. Once we see how interconnected everything is, it is no longer appropriate to think only of our own needs – we have to consider the whole, ie. the wellbeing of everyone and the planet itself. We need to learn to live differently. The current crises we face are forcing us to confront this and to move beyond self-interest. A new type of political thinking is required, a new vision, which seeks not what's best for us, or for our communities and nations, but what's best for the whole human race, the planet and for future generations.

For the last 40 years or so, growing out of the social and alternative movements of the 1960s which dealt with civil rights, women's rights, gay rights and environmental issues, there has been a huge increase in the number of people who subscribe to the new worldview values and lifestyle. The sociologist Dr Paul Ray has been studying the changing face of American culture for the last 25 years and has identified this group as 'Cultural Creatives'. In his ground-breaking book, *The Cultural Creatives: How 50 Million People Are Changing the World* (published in 2000), he describes how three subcultures exist in the US – Traditionalists, Modernists and Trans-Moderns or Cultural Creatives. Cultural Creatives are people who long for real change – 'in the direction of less stress, more health, lower consumption, more spirituality, more respect for the earth and the diversity within and among the species...'. The Cultural Creatives now comprise roughly 30 per cent of the US adult population. A set of independent surveys in Western Europe and Japan by different research teams has found that Cultural Creatives comprise as much as 35 per cent of the population. There are now reputedly

200 million Cultural Creatives. What is fascinating is that it seems to be a trend that is emerging worldwide and is embraced as much by the younger Millennium Generation as it is by the Baby Boomer Generation.

This emerging cultural phenomenon does have implications for a new kind of politics. Maybe a more inclusive and wiser kind of politics is possible, a politics based once again on the sovereignty of the people. Certainly we have to move beyond a politics of polarization. Partisan politics with its adversarial approach belongs to the old worldview. The future is about collaboration, not competition. At the same time we the voters have to re-engage in the democratic process. It is no longer appropriate for government to be left to a few politicians – we all need to be involved in a politics which is concerned with the whole. Active citizenship can build a society that's better at co-operating for the greatest good for the greatest number of its citizens. Politics is not just about leaders, power and policies – it's also about the values and attitudes, choices and behaviours that we make as citizens. We have relied too much on government that has become overly institutionalized, participating insufficiently and thereby allowing its power to increase.

Before there can be a new politics there has to be a change

in consciousness, with ordinary people becoming once again involved in the whole political process. Political protest and activism work up to a certain point – they focus people's attention on the need for change, but often there are too many conflicting and unrealistic views. There is also a need for people to change themselves.

Sit4Change, for example, is attempting to bring transformative social change to the Occupy Movement. As the internet and social media make the spread of these ideas more widespread, people are beginning to feel empowered. 'People power' is now in evidence as we become more confident in our ability to help effect change. A new politics does not come about overnight, but we are already seeing a huge sea-change which is part of a long evolutionary process which has been unfolding.

We need a re-energized, wiser form of democracy, built on trust. Jim Rough, Co-founder of the Centre for Wise Democracy, believes that many of our current crises can be solved by 'wise democracy'. In his landmark book, *Society's Breakthrough: Releasing Essential Wisdom and Virtue in All the People*, he argues that 'we the people' are the repository of collective wisdom. Tapping into that wisdom by getting everyone to work together is vital, and the best way of doing so is to create forums where people can be involved, discuss, and reflect on the best solution to problems. Jim

Rough suggests 'Creative Insight Councils' (12 people selected randomly from the electoral register) and also 'Citizens' Wisdom Councils' (12 new citizens every 4 months) as a means for people to get together on a regular basis to discuss important issues, and most importantly through dialogue to arrive at a consensus which every member supports and which is for the mutual benefit of everyone. He makes the distinction between consensus and compromise, the latter being often the worst of all possible outcomes.

Dialogue is important and involves both good listening and good discussion. We tend to be competitive as human beings and self-interested, so public conversations have a tendency to be adversarial and defensive. Most meetings are aimed at decision-making, with people trying to influence and persuade others to come round to a particular way of thinking. Jim Rough advocates 'choice-creating conversations', where people face the big issues creatively and collaboratively seeking solutions that work for everyone. By 'choice-creating' Jim Rough means that people try to understand the issues, listening to one another's feelings and needs. Through being open-minded and speaking from the heart about issues that concern them deeply, trust builds and relationships develop which can result in breakthrough solutions for problems.

There tends to be a commitment to a consensus that evolves in this, which isn't necessarily true if a decision is reached in the usual way. He makes a distinction between 'Transactional' and 'Transformational' talking. Transactional talking is more analytical and critical, whereas Transformational talking tends to combine reason, emotion and creativity. Wiser decisions tend to come from this deeper Transformational talking, This is why the Native Americans tend to have their rituals like sharing the peace pipe, passing the talking stick, and performing sacred dances to ensure that Transformational talking is employed when important decisions have to be made. Through choice-creating and Transformational talking people tend to feel empowered and realize that all problems are capable of being solved in this manner.

Jim Rough's ideas on the ways in which society can and has been organized are also valuable. The traditional way can be represented by a triangle, with the leader at the top, and regarded as more capable than others, with the populace loyal and unquestioning. Another way of organizing society is a more meritocratic way, represented by a box, where rules and laws are what matters, and the emphasis is on competing and winning. This is very much how corporations and politics tend to be oriented today, with rules and policies becoming the levers of power.

A third way of organizing society is represented by a circle, where 'we the people' are in charge with everyone actively participating. Rules and laws are still in place, but regular dialogue about what is best for everyone results in consensus on what should happen on difficult issues. Rough points out:

'Many people are already ...attempting to live according to Circle values, they feel responsible for the planet, seek consensus and look within to know what is right. They want thoughtful, respectful conversations, not debate. They want to include everyone, not just people like themselves. They want to face the big issues, not avoid them. And they want to be creative as well as rational, not just the knee-jerk implementation of more laws.' (p.218)

He suggests that the form of governance needed for the future is perhaps a box within a circle, where the box represents government, and the circle citizen deliberative councils of some form, whether Creative Insight Councils, Wisdom Councils or something similar. These methods are currently being tested by various governments, citizen groups and organizations (see www.wisedemocracy.org).

Tom Atlee also believes there is wisdom in 'the people' and that breakthrough solutions can be found for difficult problems when we are engaged in non-adversarial dialogue within a supportive democratic structure. When every voice is heard, however different the views, wiser policies can be agreed on which reflect the highest public good, and, like Jim Rough, he sees citizen deliberative councils as the means by which this can be accomplished. In his book, *The Tao of Democracy – Using Co-Intelligence to create a world that works for all*, he introduces the concept of co-intelligence – 'what intelligence would look like if we took wholeness, interconnectedness and co-creativity seriously'. He defines co-intelligence as 'the ability to organize our lives in communities and society in a way where all of us together are wiser than any of us can be alone.'

The Dalai Lama, who speaks from direct experience of having to deal with the hardest of hardline opponents, has also advocated the importance of all views being heard: 'In human societies there will always be differences of views and interests. But the reality today is that we are all interdependent and have to co-exist on this small planet. Therefore, the only sensible and intelligent way of resolving differences and clashes of interest, whether between individuals or nations, is through dialogue. The promotion of a culture of dialogue and non-violence for the future of mankind is thus an important task of the international community.'

Genuine collaborative dialogue recognizes the value of every human being, and in the process of listening and exchanging very different views, whether it is Christian with Moslem, liberal democrat with arch conservative, or the Western military with the Taliban, common ground can be reached. Each of us has only a partial view. We need to develop empathy - the ability to be able to stand in someone else's shoes. We must be willing to see the good in an opponent's position. We have to stop projecting our negative qualities on to them and seeing them as the enemy. We have to learn to reflect, and reflect to learn. We have to raise our consciousness to a higher level by becoming more self-aware, so that we understand the issues more clearly. We have to change our behaviour, which is why spirituality has to come into the political sphere. As Corinne McLaughlin says in her book, *The Practical Visionary: A new world guide to spiritual growth and social change*:

'Spirituality can help leave ego and power trips at the door and truly serve the good of the others. Politics can provide a practical arena for applying spiritual principles, such as compassion, because instant feedback is given if someone doesn't "walk the talk" – if their words are more pious than their deeds. Bringing spiritual values, such as altruism and courage, into politics can offset the immense power of moneyed interests to influence policy. It can also offset the cynicism and apathy of much of the public.' (p. 265)

We need authentic leadership dedicated to the vision of the greater good of people and the planet and to the idea of service. Successful leaders need to know themselves, and understand that they are not in power to serve their own ends and parties, but are truly concerned about the common good. Authentic leadership is not about manipulating and controlling others but about supporting, co-ordinating and nurturing people to help them grow. Developing people is important in building community. Leaders have to embody their ideals and treat everyone, including other politicians, with respect. They need to be able to draw out natural leadership and awareness in others and have the ability to be empathic.

A new politics, whether at the local, national or global level, has to be about the good of everyone as well as the environment we inhabit. It has to be about maximum participation and interaction, with individual empowerment being vital, and polarized positions have to be transcended. It needs to be able to find the common ground and synthesize the best of opposing views, arriving at a method of government that acts in the best interests of the people and the planet. This vision of creating a better politics has to draw on the wisdom inherent in us all, and for that a real change in consciousness is required. To transform politics we also have to transform ourselves. Who we are and how we relate to our fellow human beings, other species and the planet itself is reflected in the kind of politics we want for the future. 'We have to be the change we want to see in the world', to quote Gandhi. We all have to become responsible and trustworthy planetary citizens.

PART III

Conscious Evolution with the Wisdom Keys

> *Today is what it is because yesterday was what it was. And if today is like yesterday, tomorrow will be like today. If you want tomorrow to be different, you must make today different.*
>
> G. I. Gudjieff

INTRODUCTION

While prophecies can be seen as warnings of the need to change our ways, and mythology helps us understand how we can give meaning to our existence, new thinking on evolution in science and psychology shows how as human beings we are poised to transform ourselves and the world. The very crises that we are experiencing are forcing the pace of that transformation, whereby consciousness is evolving to a new and higher level. In society, in economics and even in politics, we are now seeing the signs of this evolutionary process. Hope for the future rests in our ability to transform ourselves so that we can assist the process of conscious evolution of the entire body of humanity. Inner transformation in each one of us is crucial for change to take place – there is simply no other way to bring about transformation on the scale required at this juncture.

We can see that though the world may be chaotic and confused, this process of change has been underway for some time. Whether we like it or not we are being called upon to join this transformational shift in consciousness. We may want to bury our heads in the sand, hoping the threats to our existence will go away or someone else will solve the dilemmas so that we can carry on living just as we have done. We may however have reached a point where we know that such a course is impossible, and may feel courageous enough to join the groundswell of change that is happening, and help it gather momentum fast enough to avoid catastrophe.

This change in the human psyche cannot be brought about by religious belief, although the tools of spiritual practice can help. Religion is no more than a finger pointing the way. It is for each individual to find his/her own way, though the support of like-minded people is beneficial. Religious traditions may be helpful, but they are far from necessary for the process of change. We have to look beyond the outer form of traditions and institutions and rituals to what lies at their core, the impulse for us to become truly conscious.

As many have argued, the source of our problems is we ourselves. We tend to blame everyone but ourselves, and fail to take responsibility for our part in the mess we find ourselves in. It is the over-development of the ego that sees itself as separate and more important than nature, which has resulted in a vacuum at the centre of our being, and that we constantly seek to fill through power, wealth, fame, and other distractions which bring some kind of satisfaction for a while. The development of a strong ego has been an essential stage in our development as human beings – we had to become more self-aware in order to achieve so much of the progress we have made, but this over-developed ego has to be tamed before it is too late. We are at present like adolescents, not yet fully mature human beings. Our mind is dominated by our ego and we have to release ourselves from its devious grip. Dealing with the ego is like trying to catch and tame a wild bull, so aptly illustrated by the Ten Ox-herding Pictures (or the Ten Bulls of Zen), a series of short poems in Zen Buddhism dating from the 12th century. The seeker, who has a sense of things not being quite as they appear to be, goes off to look for he knows not quite what, which is represented by the bull. He searches high and low but cannot find him. Eventually he finds the footprints of the bull so he knows that what he is looking for is right in front of him. He has to become increasingly brave and tolerant in order to catch the bull, but the bull correspondingly becomes fiercer and more uncontrollable. Much effort is made in taming him, through awareness and discipline. Gradually the bull is tamed and becomes gentle as the seeker and bull live in harmony.

THE WISDOM KEYS

The world with all its stresses and strains is a reflection
of our own minds and the dominance of the ego. The
Wisdom Keys are the personal qualities, attitudes and
behaviours we need to develop in ourselves so that the
ego is less dominant and we become less preoccupied
with our own needs and more empathic with the needs
of others and with nature as a whole. Once we use these
keys in our daily lives, our efforts to bring about change in
the world will be more effective. We can evolve and live
more authentically co-creating a whole new civilization of
human beings who live in harmony with each other and
with all life forms.

1 / Vision

Imagination is such a powerful tool. Like having a map
when we're travelling, if we have a vision of something we
want to create, it's far easier to get where we want to go.
There's a well-known story about three men working in
a quarry cutting up blocks of stone. A passer-by asks the
first man what he is doing. The first man says, 'I'm cutting
stone.' The second man answers the same question with,
'I'm earning a living.' The third man has a very different
answer – 'I'm building a cathedral.'

How do we want the future to look? We always have a choice about what we want to achieve and how we want to achieve it. Imagination has to be the starting point for our vision. If we take time to build our vision, inspiration floods in to flesh it out and show us ways of achieving our goals. The vision has to come from the deepest part of ourselves, from who we truly are. Integrity is paramount if we're to succeed – we have to initiate change inside ourselves to become 'change agents', embodying a vision of the common good. Then we need to hold our vision always in our minds, day after day, coming back to it, honouring it, however busy and distracted we may get. We'll find the energy comes and we get support from the most unexpected places, 'a thousand unseen hands' reaching out to support us. Ordinary people can accomplish the most extraordinary things when they have a vision of what they want to accomplish and stick with it, particularly when that vision is shared by other like-minded individuals.

Eileen Caddy, the spiritual teacher and author, had a vision about beginning a community at Findhorn in Scotland. Starting from very humble beginnings – a caravan park on the shores of the Moray Firth - she and her husband Peter Caddy grew some exceptionally large vegetables which attracted media attention. It also attracted thousands of visitors and has become a world-famous community and teaching centre, offering a variety of workshops and conferences.

Martin Luther King had a vision too which became a shared vision:
'I have a dream... that one day this nation will rise up and live out the true meaning of its creed: "We hold these truths to be self-evident that all men are created equal." I have a dream ... that one day on the red hills of Georgia the sons of former slaves and the sons of former slave owners will be able to sit down together at a table of brotherhood.
I have a dream...that my four children will one day live in a nation where they will not be judged by the color of their skin but by the content of their character.'
His words proved an inspiration for countless people around the world, including the current President of the USA, Obama.

Nelson Mandela also had a vision which he never lost sight of in spite of his imprisonment. His dream was that a new generation of South Africans would be free from the policy of apardheid. He believed that no sacrifice was too great on the long walk to freedom. Even within prison he fought as he had fought outside against racism and repression, always believing that he would be a free man again. And he has continued to fight for the freedom of all, white and black, oppressor and oppressed. His story of struggle, resilience and ultimate triumph remains an inspiration for us all.

Working together in a true spirit of communication and respect, so much more is achievable and the vision can become reality, transcending everyday problems and human foibles. A shared vision of the society we want   enables us to focus on what we can achieve and results in new behaviour and a new culture. We can transform our world so long as we each take responsibility for our own personal development and hold on to the vision of creating something better for the future for all of mankind.

2 / Courage

Fear is a natural response to uncertainty and danger. There's nothing wrong with feeling afraid, but fear shouldn't stop us in our tracks. We need to be bold. Courage is not the absence of fear but the triumph over it. If fear takes hold of us, it limits us and separates us, and we may even end up behaving in a way that attracts the very thing we fear to ourselves. We may fear losing our job, or our partner, we may fear getting sick, being poor, losing our looks, we almost certainly fear dying. But there are also more underlying deep-seated psychological fears that can cripple us – a fear of not being good enough, or fear of initiating a process of change and doing something different. Our fears usually stem from our wrong perceptions of a situation, something we were told in childhood by our parents or teachers perhaps, which has stayed with us and makes us feel inadequate.

We can change our perceptions by changing our thoughts. We have to live our lives fully, acting 'as if' we're not afraid, wearing a mask of boldness, and then we tend to find that we are indeed no longer afraid. In terms of facing the future collectively, we have to be bold in terms of our plans and fearless in trying to achieve them. Many individuals and groups of individuals have overcome fear and been courageous, usually when fighting for something worthwhile, whether Mahatma Gandhi in his non-violent struggle for the independence of India from the British, Mother Teresa saving the sick and caring for the dying in the slums of Calcutta, the French Resistance Movement in the Second World War, the 9/11 fire-fighters dealing with the aftermath of the terrorist attacks in New York, or the Libyan rebels overthrowing the tyrant Gadaffi.

3 / Optimism

Throughout history, from the Greek philosopher Aristotle to the modern-day motivational guru Anthony Robbins, people have written about the transformative power of optimism. Thoughts are so much more powerful than we realize - we need to be careful what we do with them, choosing optimism or negativity. A human being is supposed to have in the region of 64,000 thoughts in a single day, and all of us will have had the experience of the mind running away with itself and spiralling out of control. Our thoughts have the capacity to make us happy or sad, as the opening lines from the *Dhammapada* (a slim book of 423 verses containing the Buddha's essential teachings) remind us:

'All that we are is the result of what we have thought: all that we are is founded on our thoughts and formed of our thoughts. If a man speaks or acts with an evil thought, pain pursues him, as the wheel of the wagon follows the hoof of the ox that draws it.

All that we are is the result of what we have thought: all that we are is founded on our thoughts and formed of our thoughts. If a man speaks or acts with a pure thought, happiness pursues him like his own shadow that never leaves him.'

But how can we be optimistic in a world so confronted with crisis and where so much tragedy exists? If we're negative we'll accomplish nothing. It is always a choice we make. If we can be optimistic and hopeful, our efforts will triumph in the end, regardless of setbacks. Working to change our thought patterns brings benefits to ourselves and to those whom we come into contact with. There is no question that cultivating optimism is worthwhile.

In recent years positive psychology has gained enormous credence, and particularly the work of Dr Martin Seligman. Many psychologists claim that optimism improves health, personal effectiveness, confidence and resilience, making it easier for us to accomplish our goals. There is also objective evidence that if we are optimistic in outlook we increase our health and longevity and our cognitive flexibility and creativity, and are generally more able to be generous, kind and co-operative.

Some are critical of the whole approach of positive psychology like Barbara Ehrenreich, but she rather throws the baby out with the bathwater in her book, *Smile or Die*. Choosing to think positively and be optimistic in a situation is very different form the naïve belief that you

can have whatever you ask for, just visualize it and it will
be attracted to you. This is patently nonsense. All the
more reason for serious meditation practice, which keeps
us grounded. Just watching the breath, or the repetition
of a mantra, or a full visualization practice helps still the
mind so that we can be refreshed and renewed. Meditation
can be done anywhere and in any circumstances,
connecting us with something far deeper than our ordinary
consciousness. When we do this on a regular basis, we are
able to be more optimistic about the future in a healthy
way. In terms of facing the future collectively, we have to
make a commitment to the highest common good and
be optimistic about achieving the goals we set ourselves
whatever the obstacles that may confront us.

4 / Forgiveness

As we move into the future we can make things easier for
ourselves by lightening our load. We can try and let go of
attachments that don't really work in our best interests, in
the sense of attitudes that can hold us back and prevent us
from experiencing new and exciting opportunities. We may
be attached to our status, our appearance, our opinions,
our memories, or relationships that are unsatisfactory, or
jobs that are unfulfilling, and a host of other things. But the
less attached we are to these things, the more flexible we

are, and the more open to new possibilities.

Practising forgiveness also frees us up. Letting go of old wounds, disappointments, loss, injustices, betrayals, rather than allowing them to gnaw away at us, means that a different kind of energy can fill us. Forgiveness improves health and relationships. All the religious traditions of the world have emphasized the need for forgiveness. If we're consumed by anger or resentment, we're doing ourselves a disservice – we're prisoners of the past, replaying old tapes, and unavailable to both the present and the future. But if we can rise above the pain of the past, wounds are healed and we are more able to give freely of ourselves and be available for the future.

This is also true for families, communities, races, whole societies and nations. Archbishop Desmond Tutu presided over the Truth and Reconciliation Commission in South Africa. Rather than vengeance, and the continuance of hatred and racism, forgiveness, healing and compassion were the goals, and in order for reconciliation, the truth of what had happened had to be exposed. Just as old wounds have to be opened up and cleaned before healing can take place, once the truth of a situation is evident for all then forgiveness can happen and healing begin.

Forgiveness, and a change of heart, results in a radical transformation of ourselves. Only when we truly forgive wrongs that have been committed can there be peace. Our need for peace, individually and collectively, can be fulfilled only when we choose to forgive rather than continue in turmoil with thoughts of anger and revenge.

5 / Trust

Trust is essential in society and is linked with a sense of purpose and meaning. As we look towards the future, there's so little we can feel any certainty about and put our trust in, except the process of change itself. We certainly can't put our trust in governments, the stock markets, banks or the kind of things our society seems to value – money, power, celebrity, beauty or youth.

We need instead to have faith in something beyond all these things, to trust that there exists a power greater than ourselves, whether we call it nature, the universe, Spirit, god, whatever term we feel at ease with. Only the cynic refuses to acknowledge that there is some greater power in the universe, while the agnostic admits that he/she does not know. But when we allow ourselves to feel that reverence for a creative power at the heart of life and to trust the unfolding of life's evolutionary process, faith grows. We grow stronger because of it and are more able to deal with whatever challenges lie ahead, because we trust that what happens in life is for our growth.

Growth isn't something we think about very often, in fact we don't think about it very much at all when we're happy. It's far more likely that pain and suffering teach us what we need to know to become wiser human beings and more at peace with ourselves. When we look back on our disappointments, losses and tragedies (and no life is without them), we usually find that we have learned a great deal from them and are able to be more compassionate to others. That is why trusting life to unfold in the way it does is something we need to cultivate.

6 / Attention

Attention means giving ourselves wholly to something and when we pay very close attention to something, then we are living in the present moment, the Now. Unfortunately we tend to live our lives through memory and anticipation, rather than living in the present. We hark back to the past going over something that may have happened moments, hours or even years before, and we think about the future either worrying about what may happen or day-dreaming about some future event whether it's what we're doing after work or the holiday we have planned for next year. Rarely are we able to live in the present, when the mind ceases its endless chatter and we feel a sense of peace and clarity.

If we focus on the Now, there are no problems that we cannot deal with, and we find we have huge resources of energy to accomplish what we want to do. When the task in hand commands our full attention, whether it's baking bread, gardening, making a pot, playing in an orchestra, or decorating a hall for our community, if we carefully observe the tasks we're engaged in, then we completely forget anything else except what we're doing.

Blaise Paschal, the seventeenth-century theologian, claimed, 'All men's miseries derive from being unable to sit quiet in a room.' The mystics have always understood the need to pay attention and the value of silence. The Desert Fathers went out into the wilderness, to live alone, free from distractions; the rishis, or holy men of India, went into forests or caves; monk and nuns retreated to the cloisters. We may not feel that we want to be that extreme! But if we want to live differently, if we want peace of mind for ourselves, and a more peaceful world, then taking time out to be silent and pay attention to what's going on inside ourselves is vital. We seem to have no time for ourselves – there's too much to do, we live as though we're immortal, running ever faster, we're addicted to things and experiences that don't give us the lasting satisfaction we crave. This is *samsara* - the daily round we're caught up in, a kind of incompleteness that we sense, the hole at the centre of our being, the unsatisfactory nature of so much of what we call our lives. We need to live in the present moment, the here and now. We need to stop, slow down and breathe. Our breath is very much a reflection of the state we're in. Periods of just 'being' is what we need, as opposed to always doing or being stimulated by something. If we live in the present moment, accepting it just as it is, without judgment, and let it unfold to the next moment, we will find a greater peace within ourselves and also have access to a place of wisdom and inspiration. Artists, writers, poets and composers have often testified to this need for silence for creativity to flow, and be able to produce their work.

We may not feel we want to give huge amounts of time to sitting still and paying attention, but if we set aside time on a regular basis, a new awareness develops. As we become more at peace through this practice, then we are more able to manifest it in our lives, and then we can begin to make a difference in the world. We are able to listen to others more fully, whether it's our spouse, our boss, a friend, or the still small voice within. We have to give space to truly listen; we can't be doing something else at the same time if we're truly to give our full attention.

7 / Gratitude

Life is never easy – no one lives a completely charmed life, no matter who they are. Things go wrong, turn out different from what we had expected, 'shit happens', as they say; and as a result of the various crises we're going through, probably none of us has escaped unscathed. And maybe worse could lie ahead – we just don't know. It's easy to get downcast and depressed about the future, but in taking time to 'count our blessings' and remember the positive things about our lives, even in the most difficult of circumstances, things begin to look different.

When we truly appreciate what we have in life (and we in the West have much to be grateful for), we appreciate the preciousness of life itself. We know from heart rate variability (HRV) or heart rhythms) that sustained positive emotions like gratitude have beneficial effect, producing a higher degree of coherence within the heart's rhythmic activity, as well as throughout other systems in the body from blood pressure to the digestive system.

It is just as important however to be appreciative of the difficult times in our life too, for they have provided us with the opportunity to learn and grow.

8 / *Compassion*

Compassion requires us to treat others as we would ourselves wish to be treated – the so-called Golden Rule. All the great humanitarians and teachers of different spiritual persuasions have stressed the importance of compassion, which is about having empathy for all forms of life, human or otherwise, with whom we share a deep bond. Compassion requires us to be less self-centred and to recognize this connection. Compassion is a natural instinct – our heart goes out to people who are suffering. Sometimes however it is difficult to feel love and empathy for others if we're anxious or unhappy ourselves, and our circumstances seem dark and hopeless? How can we feel love for those who have hurt us, or compassion for those who commit terrible crimes? These are difficult issues, but the new consciousness requires that we let go of the ego's attachment to negativity. Negative emotions are harmful whereas positive thoughts and emotions profoundly affect are health and well-being

To practise compassion, we start with ourselves. We take

time to nurture ourselves with life-enhancing behaviour, increasing the amount of love we feel towards ourselves, and this results in better outcomes in our life. There is nothing narcissistic or selfish about this. Unless we feel good about ourselves, and truly accept who we really are, we're unlikely to feel compassion for others. When we are happy with the way we are, then we can more readily love our neighbours as ourselves, we are more able to empathize with another's pain, or begin to understand how deprivation and violence beget unspeakable acts. We can start by making our 'neighbour' everyone we meet – the checkout girl, the homeless person, the stranger – a smile and acknowledgment, a kind word, a helping hand – these things make a difference. Compassion requires practice, and the more we are able to cultivate it, the better it is for our mental, emotional, spiritual and physical health. In fact, every act of compassion has a chemical impact on the brain, since natural opiates are released and help lift our mood. By practising compassion frequently our brain actually changes because we flex and enlarge the compassion-producing areas of the brain, just as we improve our body muscles by exercising them regularly.

The Institute of Heart Math has conducted research showing the physiological and psychological effects of both compassion and anger (1995). Heart-focused, sincere, positive feeling states boost the immune system while negative emotions suppress the immune system. There is every reason therefore to be more compassionate and help to relieve the suffering of our fellow human beings whoever they are. Getting people to understand this and to commit to practising lies behind initiatives like the Charter for Compassion and the Greater Good Science Center at the University of California, Berkeley.

9 / Service

Without a sense of purpose in life, it's unlikely that we will feel fulfilled and become truly mature human beings. Today's society has an unhealthy emphasis on consumption, achievement and status. Sadly we often find ourselves climbing the wrong ladder, wondering what life is all about. Most human beings want to be happy once their basic needs are fulfilled, but how do we find real happiness as opposed to something that is fleeting? When we look outside ourselves we're most likely only going to experience a short-lived sense of happiness. We're more likely to feel happy if we have a sense of purpose in our lives that goes deeper than the ego's wants and desires. And that requires a deeper understanding of why we think we're here. Ultimately, it's the connection to a larger reality – the whole, the universe, God, Spirit, whatever we choose to call it that gives a sense of meaning to our lives. And with that as a backdrop we're more likely to choose to commit ourselves to helping to make others' lives better. In using our skills and talents to the best of our capacity to serve others we are fulfilling our lives' purpose, and there is no more meaningful work.

Kahlil Gibran, the Lebanese author of *The Prophet* says: 'Work is love made visible.' This is very much what karma yoga is (one of the four paths of yoga). Literally karma yoga means 'union through action'. We have to act without being attached to the fruits of our action. The great dialogue on this is in the *Bhagavad Gita* (part of the Hindu epic, the *Mahabharata*), when Prince Arjuna is talking to Krishna on the eve of a great dynastic battle. Krishna tells Arjuna that he must fight. By acting as an instrument of God and not being attached to the outcome of his actions, then he is performing his duty. Similar ideas can be found in other religious traditions eg. the Parable of the Talents in the New Testament. Right livelihood is one of the Eight Precepts of the path of Buddhism, and is about making one's work helpful to other people. Exploiting others, unethical investment and an obsession with profit, and using up the earth's resources without replacing them have no place in the world of the future.

We can play our part by keeping our own house in order, and doing everything we can to help others. This does not necessarily mean that we rush off to go and help earthquake victims, or feed the hungry and homeless or work with the sick and dying, though some are equipped to do just that. Each of us can make a meaningful contribution through the way we live our daily lives, through supporting appropriate charities, by making the right choices in the workplace and how we spend our leisure time, and through how we relate to all those we come into contact with. Volunteering, or simply giving of ourselves and our time when someone needs it, and going that extra mile – that is service.

10 / Simplicity

Our overall approach to living and consuming is changing. In the developed world we're beginning to recognize that we've become enslaved by the consumer culture and have sacrificed too much of our time and energy to it. We have placed too high a value on material possessions and made life too complicated by having too many expectations and commitments. I'm not suggesting that we be as radical as the millionaire who gave away every penny of his three million pound fortune, or the woman in Germany who has lived voluntarily without money for the last thirteen years, but we should ask ourselves, how much do we actually need?

The material improvements in our lives in the western world over the last fifty years have often been at the cost of enjoying the simple things of life. The rise of material affluence has resulted in a huge increase in depression and anxiety. Rather than satisfying our needs, we're constantly trying to satisfy our wants, and the problem with that is that there is always a desire for something else once one desire has been satisfied. The truth however is that simple pleasures bring greater satisfaction than material possessions, simple past times don't cost the earth, and simple food is likely to keep us healthier.

Increasingly people are realizing that a more balanced approach to living is infinitely more satisfying. Simpler and greener approaches to living are becoming part of everyday life and culture for many – from organic gardening and farming, to healthier cooking, use of solar energy, running small businesses from home, to making things and buying second-hand. People see the sense in being debt-free, living more cheaply, and having more free time. And as Gandhi put it so wisely – 'there is enough for each man's need but not enough for each man's greed.'

EPILOGUE

In the final stages of preparing this book for publication
I continue to feel an enormous sense of hope about
the times we're living through.   In spite of the horrors
continuing in Syria, Afghanistan and the Sudan, in spite
of the social and economic problems which continue to
confront us, and in spite of the ever-increasing changes in
climates around the world, something positive is happening.

Millions of people know in their hearts that things have to
change and that we can build a different kind of future. All
is not lost. The crises we face are forcing us to change our
ways. The new social media not only connect us and tell
us what is happening on our small planet, but also help us
to see how we might change by making available a wealth
of ideas and opportunities. Each one of us can take up
the challenge of change, and consciously evolve as life has
always evolved, by co-operating and working together, so
that our world becomes the better place that it is destined
to be.

By a strange coincidence, whilst I was considering the
date for publication, I discovered that on 5/6 June a
rare astrological and astronomical event is taking place.
This happens approximately every 121 years, when the

planet Venus passes across the face of the Sun. Such an event in the past seems to have coincided with shifts in consciousness. A wonderful omen perhaps, with Venus being the planet of love, for a more co-operative, caring and peaceful world at this momentous stage of our evolution.

April 8th 2012

BIBLIOGRAPHY

Atlee, Tom, *The Tao of Democracy: Using Co-Intelligence to Create A World that Works for All*, The Writers Collective, 2003.

Christakis, Nicholas A. and Fowler, James H., *Connected: The Surprising Power of Our Social Networks and How They Shape Our Lives*, HarperCollins, 2010.

Campbell, Joseph with Moyers, Bill, *The Power of Myth*, Doubleday, 1998.

Campbell, Joseph, *The Hero with a Thousand Faces*, Fontana, 1993.

Eisler, Rianne, *The Chalice and the Blade*, Thorsons, 1987.

Florida, Richard, *The Great Reset: How the Post-Crash Economy Will Change the Way We Live and Work*, HarperCollins, 2010.

Frazer, James George, *The Golden Bough*, Oxford World's Classics, 1994.

Gerhardt, Sue, *The Selfish Society: How We All Forgot to Love One Another and Made Money Instead*, Simon & Schuster, 2010

Gerzema, John and D'Antonio, Michael, *Spend Shift: How the Post-Crisis Values Revolution is Changing the Way We Buy, Sell, and Live*, Jossey-Bass, 2011.

Gimbutas, Marija, *The Language of the Goddess*, Harper & Row, 1989.

Gimbutas, Marija, *The Civilization of the Goddess*, Harper & Row, 1991.

Grant, John, *Co-Opportunity: Join Up for a Sustainable, Resilient, Prosperous World*, Wiley, 2010.

Gratton, Lynda, *The Shift: The Future of Work is Already Here*, HarperCollins, 2011.

Greene, Liz, *Relating: An Astrological Guide to Living with Others on a Small Planet*, Coventure, 1977.

Hardy, Jean, *A Wiser Politics*, O Books, 2011.

Hawken, Paul, *Blessed Unrest: How the Largest Social Movement in History is Restoring Grace, Justice, and Beauty to the World*, Penguin Books, 2007.

Heinberg, Richard, *Memories and Visions of Paradise: Exploring the Universal Myth of a Lost Golden Age*, Tarcher, 1989.

Hopkins, Rob, *The Transition Handbook: From Oil Dependency to Local Resilience*, Green Books, 2008.

Howell, Alice O., *The Heavens Declare: Astrological Ages and the Evolution of Consciousness*, Quest Books, 2006

Hubbard, Barbara Marx, *Conscious Evolution: Awakening the Power of Our Social Potential*, New World Library, 1998.

Hutton, Will, *Them and Us: Changing Britain – Why We Need a Fair Society*, Little, Brown, 2010

Jackson, Tim, *Prosperity without Growth: Economics for a Finite Planet*, Earthscan, 2009.

Judith, Anodea, *Waking the Global Heart: Humanity's Rite of Passage from the Love of Power to the Power of Love*, Elite Books, 2006.

Korten, David C., *Agenda for a New Economy: From Phantom Wealth to Real Wealth*, 2nd edition, 2010, Berrett-Koehler Publishers Inc.

Layard, Richard, *Happiness: Lessons from a New Science*, Penguin Books, 2003.

LeGrain, Philippe, *Aftershock: Reshaping the World Economy after the Crisis*, Little, Brown, 2010.

Lipton, Bruce H. And Bhaerman, Steve, *Spontaneous Evolution: Our Positive Future*, Hay House, 2009.

McLaughlin, Corinne and Davidson, Gordon, *Spiritual Politics: Changing the World from the Inside Out*, Ballantine Books, 1994.

McLaughlin, Corinne with Davidson, Gordon, *The Practical Visionary: A New World Guide to Spiritual Growth and Social Change*, Unity House, 2010.

McTaggart, Lynne, *The Field: The Quest for the Secret Force of the Universe*, HarperCollins, 2001.

McTaggart, Lynne, *The Intention Experiment: Using Your Thoughts to Change Your Life and the World*, Simon & Schuster, 2007.

McTaggart, Lynne, *The Bond: Connecting Through the Space Between Us*, Hay House, 2011.

Meade, Michael, *The World Behind the World: Living at the Ends of Time*, Greenfire Press, 2008.

O'Dea, James, *Creative Stress: A Path for Evolving Souls Living Through Personal and Planetary Upheaval*, Pioneer Imprints, 2010.

Ray, Paul H, and Anderson, Sherry Ruth, *The Cultural Creatives: How 50 Million People Are Changing the World*, Harmony Books, 2000.

Ray, Paul H., *The New Political Compass: The New Progressives are In-Front, Deep Green, Against Big Business and Globalization, and Beyond Left vs. Right*, free download, 2002.

Ricard, Matthieu, *Happiness: A Guide to Developing Life's Most Important Skill*, Atlantic Books, 2003.

Rogers, Peter and Leal, Susan, *Running out of Water: The Looming Crisis and Solutions to Conserve Our Most Precious Resource*, Palgrave, MacMillan, 2010.

Rough, Jim, *Society's Breakthrough; Releasing the Essential Wisdom and Virtue in All the People*, 1st Books Library, 2002.

Russell, Peter, *The Awakening Earth: Our Next Evolutionary Leap*, RKP, 1982.

Rushby, Kevin, *Paradise: A History of the Idea that Rules the World*, Constable & Robinson, 2006.

Sahtouris, Elisabet, *Earthdance: Living Systems in Evolution*, free download, 1999.

Seligman, Martin E.P., *Authentic Happiness: Using the New Positive Psychology to Realize Your Potential for Lasting Fulfilment*, Nicholas Brealey Publishing, 2003.

Seligman, Martin E. P., *Flourish: A New Understanding of Happiness and Well-Being – And How to Achieve Them*, Nicholas Brealey Publishing, 2011.

Sivaraksa, Sulak, *The Wisdom of Sustainability: Buddhist Economics for the 21st Century*, Souvenir Press, 2009.

Sounds True, *The Mystery of 2012: Predictions, Prophecies and Possibilities*, Sounds True Inc, 2007.

Taylor, Steve, *The Fall: The Insanity of the Ego in Human History and the Dawning of a New Era*, O Books, 2005.

Thompson, Damian, *The End of Time: Faith and Fear in the Shadow of the Millennium*, Vintage, 1999

Tolle, Eckhart, *A New Earth: Awakening to Your life's Purpose*, Hodder & Stoughton, 2005.

Trainer, Ted, *The Simpler Way: Working for Transition from Consumer Society to a Simpler, More Co-operative, Just and Ecologically Sustainable Society*, free download, 2011.

Wheatley, Margaret and Frieze, Deborah, *Walk Out Walk On: A Learning Journey Into Communities Daring to Live the Future Now*, 2011, Berrett-Koehler Publishers Inc.

Wilber, Ken, *A Brief History of Everything*, 2nd edn, Gateway, 2001.

Wilkinson, Richard and Pickett, Kate, *The Spirit Level: Why Equality is Better for Everyone*, 2009, Allen Lane.

RESOURCES/WEBSITES

www.evolutionshift.com – a future look at today by futurist David Houle

www.greatergood.berkeley.edu - The Greater Good Science Center studies the psychology, sociology and neuroscience of wellbeing, and teaches skills that foster a thriving, resilient and compassionate society

www.wiserearth.org - the social network for sustainability

www.charterforcompassion.org - a co-operative effort to restore both compassionate thinking and compassionate action to the centre of religious, moral and political life

www.worldchanging.com - dedicated to solutions-based journalism about the planetary future

www.positivenews.org.uk - aims to inform, inspire, and empower its readers while helping create a more responsible and balanced media

www.positivenewsus.org - news from around the world in the area of sustainability, social equality, education and happiness

www.findhorn.org - spiritual community, learning centre, eco-village

www.alternatives.org.uk – dedicated to exploring ways of living and being. Regular talks and workshops

www.heartmath.com - aims to help establish heart-based living and global coherence by inspiring people to connect with the intelligence and guidance of their own hearts

www.humanitysteam.org - 'a civil rights movement for the soul', set up by author Neale Donald Walsh

www.theshiftnetwork.com - aims to empower a global movement of people who are creating an evolutionary shift of consciousness

www.worldshift2012.org - a global social network dedicated to sustainable transformation and conscious evolution

www.theshiftmovie.com - a movie in the making, documenting the greatest social transformation in human history – YouTube

www.transitionnetwork.org - supports community-led responses to climate change and shrinking supplies of cheap energy, building resilience and happiness

www.transitionculture.org - 'an evolving exploration into the head, heart and hands of energy descent' blog by Rob Hopkins, co-founder of the Transition Network

www.yes!magazine.org - empowers people with the vision and tools to create a healthy planet and vibrant communities

www.anhglobal.org - Alliance for a New Humanity – creating alliances toward one world that honours life and builds an awareness of humanity's interconnectedness

www.walkoutwalkon.net - a learning journey into communities daring to live the future now

www.auroville.org - a universal city in the making, where people of all countries can live in peace and progressive harmony

www.damanhur.org - eco-society based on ethical and spiritual values

www.livingeconomiesforum.org - 'The old economy of greed and dominion is dying. A new economy of life and partnership is struggling to be born' - the online home of author David Korten.

www.barbaramarxhubbard.com -Foundation for Conscious Evolution

www.transformingthrough2012 - leading perspectives on the new global paradigm

www.peace2012.net - creating a peaceful and positive 2012

www.wisdomuniversity.org - providing learning experiences that catalyze the enlargement of the soul and inspire resilient learning communities to thrive

www.wisedemocracy.org   - Center for Wise Democracy, where all people participate in one conversation, address the most important issues, and creatively determine solutions that work for everyone

www.avaaz.org - the campaigning community bringing people-powered politics to decision-making worldwide

www.ic.org - Intentional Communities Directory – serving the growing communities movement, providing resources for starting a community, finding a community home, living in community and creating more community in your life

www.opencentre.org - New York's leading centre of holistic learning and world culture

www.eomega.org   - Omega Institute for Holistic Studies, educational retreat centre offering workshops and conferences to provide hope and healing for individuals and society by awakening the best in the human spirit

www.equalitytrust.org.uk - campaigns to gain the widest public and political understanding og the harm caused by inequality

www.actionforhappiness.org - a movement for positive social change

www.theyoungfoundation.org - brings together insights, innovations and entrepreneurship to meet social needs, working across the UK and internationally

www.slowmovement.com - aims to address the issue of 'time poverty' through making connections

www.neweconomics.org - independent think-tank concerned with real economic well-being